The Magnificent Obsession

The Magnificent Obsession

Keegan, Sir John Hall, Newcastle and Sixty Million Pounds

Colin Malam

BLOOMSBURY

First published in Great Britain 1997

Bloomsbury Publishing Plc, 38 Soho Square, London W1V 5DF

Copyright © 1997 by Colin Malam

The moral right of the author has been asserted

PICTURE SOURCES

Allsport: pages 4 *top*; 8 *bottom left* and *bottom centre*
BSkyB Ltd: page 5 *top*
Mirror Syndication International: pages 1; 2 *top*;
4 *bottom*; 7; 8 *top* and *bottom right*
North News & Pictures: pages 2 *bottom*; 5 *bottom*
PA News: page 6
Stewart Bonney Agency: page 3

A CIP catalogue record for this book
is available from the British Library

ISBN 0 7475 3750 X

10 9 8 7 6 5 4 3 2 1

Typeset by Hewer Text Composition Services, Edinburgh
Printed by Clays Ltd, St Ives plc

CONTENTS

Acknowledgements   vii
Introduction   1

1. Genesis   5
2. The Wilderness Years   17
3. The Second Coming   33
4. Ascension   49
5. Onwards and Upwards   63
6. Europe and Andy   73
7. Torment   85
8. The Apocalypse   97
9. The Epilogue   113
10. John and Kevin   127
11. In Retrospect   139
12. The Geordie Nation   161
13. The Future   177

ACKNOWLEDGEMENTS

Since this book had to be written against a rather tight deadline, the help received from others was particularly valuable. I would therefore like to offer my deepest gratitude to all of those people connected with Newcastle United in one way or another who willingly gave their time to impart information and express opinions about the period in question. I am especially indebted to John Gibson, executive sports editor of the *Newcastle Evening Chronicle*, who was my expert and unfailingly patient guide through the trickier parts of the terrain. If there are any factual errors to be found here, they are mine and not his.

The assistance of the Telegraph Group's Stephanie Pryor was also invaluable. Without her computer expertise and general efficiency it would have been immeasurably more difficult to get the manuscript to the publishers. At Bloomsbury, the encouragement and patience of David Reynolds and Monica Macdonald were greatly appreciated. Thanks are also due to Sir John Hall's secretary, Louise Roberts; and my sports editor at the *Sunday Telegraph*, Colin Gibson, who did everything he could to help me fit the writing of the book into a busy working schedule at the start of a new football season.

Others who helped get the project underway and/or lighten the load include my agent, John Pawsey; football correspondent of the *Independent on Sunday* Ian Ridley; football columnist for the *Sunday Telegraph* Patrick Barclay; the man who has made the *Rothman's Football Yearbook* the 'bible' of the game, Jack Rollin; the *Guardian*'s award-winning sports columnist Paul Hayward; Alison Sharpe of Deloitte & Touche; Jack Carroll of the *Sunday Telegraph*; and, last but not least, my wife and sons.

I would also like to acknowledge the varying degrees of assistance I derived from the following publications: *Geordie Messiah – The Keegan Years* by Alan Oliver; *Kevin Keegan – Black & White* by John Moynihan; *Kevin Keegan – Portrait of a Superstar* by John Gibson; *Dalglish – My Autobiography* by Kenny Dalglish and Henry Winter; the *Deloitte & Touche Annual Review of Football Finance* edited by Gerry Boon; and, of course, the *Rothman's Football Yearbook*.

INTRODUCTION

It was, to borrow shamelessly from Dickens, the best of times and the worst of times. Emotionally, in this tale of one unusual city and its football team, Kevin Keegan took Newcastle United and their fans to the heights and to the depths during the five years he managed the club between 1992 and 1997. It was, by turns, both exhilarating and draining; but mostly exhilarating. It was also, by common consent, one of the most remarkable periods in the history of English football – almost revolutionary, in fact.

That was largely because Keegan attempted to win the biggest prizes by flying in the face of the received wisdom on tactics . . . And so nearly succeeded. At a time when it was generally accepted that a sound defence and a degree of caution had to be the watchwords of a successful side, Keegan preferred the old adage that promotes attack as the best form of defence. Astonishingly, the Newcastle manager tried to prove it possible to win the major prizes by playing all-out attacking football, all the time.

Given the taxing nature of the long and crowded English season, Keegan's was a particularly bold concept, to say the least. Not that his intention, it would seem, was to bring about a tactical revolution – it was more a question of obeying his own instincts as a former striker and of keeping faith with the Newcastle fans and their enduring taste for entertaining football. But if Keegan's team had managed to win the Premiership, as they so nearly did, there is no knowing where it all might have led. At the very least, his Newcastle could be said to have symbolized the world-wide appeal of the newly enriched, increasingly cosmopolitan Premier League. That is to say, their unrelenting willingness to attack was so risky, so susceptible to error and the potentially devastating counter-attack, that the spectator was treated to a truly entertaining spectacle.

Keegan always justified his team's forthright approach by insisting that they were playing in the way the Toon Army, as the loyal and passionate Newcastle fans are known, wanted to see Newcastle play. His view was based on the strong, almost mystical bond that had developed between him and the supporters during the two years – the final ones of his playing career – he had spent at St James' Park in the early 1980s. He believed implicitly that the fans wanted attacking football, and he was determined they should have it. Brought up in a mining community himself, Keegan seemed to know intuitively that the citizens of Newcastle needed lifting out of the deadening cycle of industrial decline represented by the systematic closure of mines and shipyards in the North East since the Second World War.

Indeed, the reawakening of Newcastle United under the management of Keegan and the chairmanship of Sir John Hall, two equally dynamic men, could be seen as a vital part of the impressive economic and social regeneration that has taken place on Tyneside during the 1980s and 1990s. Sir John, who not only made his own vast fortune but also injected millions into the local economy – he built the massive indoor shopping mall, the Metro Centre, at Gateshead, just across the river from Newcastle – certainly regards the revitalization of the area's sport as being as important as anything else in the restoration of the populace's self-confidence.

Some degree of self-doubt must have crept back into the Geordie psyche, therefore, after watching Newcastle squander an apparently unassailable twelve-point lead at the top of the Premiership in the latter part of the 1995–96 season. The television images following each successive, sickening setback, of stunned, disbelieving and tearful fans in black and white favours, will linger in the memory quite as long as the thrilling

INTRODUCTION

play which had taken Newcastle so far ahead of Manchester United, the eventual champions, for most of the season.

There was no lack of sympathy for the Toon Army around the rest of the country or the world, since Newcastle had become just about everyone else's second favourite team by then. Derek Fazackerley, first-team coach for much of the five-year period in question, remembers the supporters of other clubs stopping Keegan in the street on away trips and telling him how much they enjoyed watching his side play. Labour councillor Terry Cooney, who represents the Fenham Ward close to St James' Park, recalls a Peruvian politician raving to him about English football in general and Newcastle United in particular when they met at a conference in Amsterdam.

Such popularity and fame were major achievements in themselves. For when Keegan took over at St James' Park in February 1992, Newcastle had been in serious danger of dropping into the old Third Division of the Football League for the first time in more than a hundred years as a professional club. After yo-yoing between the top two divisions for most of the post-war period, one of the biggest clubs in the North East, that hotbed of the game, appeared to be in terminal decline.

Yet only two years later Newcastle were back with the big boys and challenging for the championship of the newly formed Premier League, the old First Division in autonomous, money-spinning disguise. It was an achievement made all the more remarkable by the fact that Keegan not only had no previous experience of management or coaching, but had also been out of football for all of the eight years since his retirement as a Newcastle player.

It was not as though he made up for the deficiency, either, by recruiting experience. Terry McDermott, the former Liverpool, Newcastle and England team-mate he asked to help him, was as much of a managerial novice as Keegan was. While Keegan was playing golf and generally living the lotus life in southern Spain during his time out of the game, McDermott had been no closer to football than a business supplying the VIP catering at racecourses.

In truth, Newcastle's appointment of Keegan as their manager was an enormous gamble. Not least because it was carried out in clandestine fashion by a section of the board at a time when the fierce, protracted battle for control of the club was reaching its climax. If Keegan had not been such an instant hit, the triumphant faction headed by Sir John Hall might have found itself facing some very awkward questions.

Quite rightly, the Hall–Keegan liaison came to be seen by the deprived fans of Newcastle United as a dream ticket, capable of transporting them to hitherto inaccessible areas of success and delight. The combination of Hall's money and Keegan's charisma – not to mention the sheer drive of those two determined and strong-willed characters – certainly transformed the club beyond recognition. But success and delight? Thereby hangs a tale ...

1

GENESIS

Kevin Keegan could be said to have started managing Newcastle United on 19 August 1982, ten full years before he took control of the team officially. This earlier date was the point at which Keegan decided St James' Park was where he wanted to spend the final years of his distinguished playing career. It was also the point at which he began to exert a powerful influence over the club and establish that extraordinary rapport with the Newcastle supporters which helped to shape and define his unusual and distinctive managerial style and ethos a decade later.

Throughout the five years in which Keegan, as manager, transformed the battered flagship of the Geordies from a rudderless craft into one of the most powerful battle-cruisers afloat, he used the passion and the loyalty of the fans as a guiding star. He knew from first hand experience just how much they craved success, how much they appreciated good, attacking football – and he clearly resolved to satisfy the longings of the people who had welcomed him and worshipped him during his last two years as a player.

While there are those who would argue, with some justification, that Keegan was simply doing what came naturally and obeying his instincts as a former striker, it would be entirely wrong to dismiss offhand the repeated insistence that under his management Newcastle played unrestrained, attacking football because it was what the supporters wanted to see. No set of fans is closer to its team, and there was an unusually strong bond between Keegan and the Toon Army.

Not surprisingly, the fans idolized him because he chose first to excite and uplift them with his presence at a time when he was twice-European Footballer of the Year and captain of the England team. In fact, Keegan had not long returned from the Spanish finals of the 1982 World Cup when he decided that he wanted a move from Southampton, who had pulled off quite a coup two years earlier by paying Hamburg £420,000 to bring him back into English football.

The Hampshire club, then managed by the innovative, go-getting Lawrie McMenemy, had finished seventh in the former First Division at the end of the 1981–82 season, after leading the table at the turn of the year. They had slipped out of contention due to Southampton's financial inability to strengthen the squad, and this irked Keegan. He was also depressed after personally disappointing World Cup finals in which a troublesome back injury had restricted him to a brief appearance in England's last match, a goalless second-phase game against Spain during which he had missed a late scoring chance he would normally have put away with his eyes closed.

So he came home from Madrid in the summer of 1982 looking for a psychological lift, a new challenge. McMenemy was not pleased to hear his star player ask for a transfer only a year after signing a new contract, but he knew the affluent, determined Keegan well enough to realize that he would simply have walked out of the game if Southampton had refused to let him go. 'No one – and I repeat, no one – wanted Kevin to leave,' said McMenemy at the time. 'Money was never mentioned when Keegan first came to me and said he wanted a new club. He made it quite clear that he hadn't the impetus to start again with us, to grind along for another season. I blame the World Cup for that. It changed things for him.'

Even then, at thirty-one, Keegan was still enough of a player and a personality to have had his pick of clubs. In addition to all his other accolades he had finished the 1981–82 season as winner of the Golden Boot award for the leading scorer in the former First Division and as the Professional Footballers' Association Player of the Year. Manchester United certainly wanted him, but he could not agree personal terms with the celebrated First Division club and chose instead to join Newcastle, who were then just over halfway through a six-year spell in the former Second Division and decidedly hard up.

'We're in heaven – we've got Kevin,' quipped club secretary Russell Cushing excitedly at the start of the press conference to announce the signing, and his joyful mantra was echoed all over Tyneside. No one could quite believe that such a famous footballer would, of his own free will, choose to join a club that had shown little ambition for years and appeared to have a limited future. It was a demonstration of faith that was to stand Keegan in very good stead, both then and later.

'From the moment I met Newcastle's officials and shook hands, I knew that was it,' Keegan said. 'I only talked to two clubs, Manchester United and Newcastle United, but I could have talked to thirty. I knew Newcastle wanted me, and I have never felt so excited in a long time – not since I first met Bill Shankly.' The comparison with the legendary manager of Liverpool, who had given Keegan his first big chance by buying him from Scunthorpe United, was flattering enough to suggest an already well-developed gift for public relations.

The clinch, in this context, was Keegan's revelation that his father, Joe, had been a Geordie miner who moved the family down to Armthorpe near Doncaster – where Kevin was born – in search of work. Better still, his mine inspector grandfather, Frank, was remembered as a hero in County Durham, where he and his rescue team had saved the lives of thirty men and a pony in the West Stanley pit disaster of 1909. Thus Keegan was taken into every heart on Tyneside before he had even kicked a ball. As John Gibson, executive sports editor of the local evening paper, the *Chronicle*, observes: 'It was a case of, "Oh, Kevin's an adopted Geordie. He's really one of us!" And that was a great help.' Nevertheless Gibson, ever the hard-bitten newspaperman, does add: 'Kevin was so good at PR, so good at getting the perfect setting for any situation, you always had the feeling that if he went to Alaska he'd have a bloody Eskimo in his wardrobe!'

THE MAGNIFICENT OBSESSION

The mixture of delight and disbelief experienced on Tyneside as a result of Keegan's startling decision to join Newcastle is conveyed vividly by Gibson. 'It was a huge surprise,' he recalls, 'because Kevin was England captain and Newcastle were then a dreadful Second Division club going absolutely nowhere and going there fast. So even though the fee of £100,000 was controlled by a clause in his contract with Southampton, the fans couldn't believe that Newcastle would get him. Particularly as the other club supposedly after him was Manchester United.'

Gibson, a Geordie who has supported Newcastle since 1950 and covered their progress lovingly, objectively and trenchantly for the local paper since 1966, remembers the Keegan signing with pleasure on both counts. 'There had been great speculation about whether Kevin was going to come or whether he wasn't. As it happened, Lawrie McMenemy was a very good friend of mine – he had been the coach at Gateshead at the start of his great career when I covered them as a cub reporter, and we got on so well that he had come to my twenty-first birthday party.

'Anyway, with Newcastle refusing to confirm or deny the Keegan story and everybody wondering what would happen, Lawrie phoned me at the *Chronicle* from Amsterdam airport, through which Southampton happened to be passing on a pre-season tour. He told me Keegan had just caught a plane to Newcastle, and we got a page-one exclusive on his arrival. The moment the paper came out, people started queueing up at St James' Park for season tickets. Then there was a huge press conference at the Gosforth Park Hotel, where Russell Cushing coined his famous phrase about the club being in heaven because they'd got Kevin.'

It was a surprisingly imaginative move by a board not noted for bold initiatives. Led by chairman Stan Seymour, they gave admirable support to what at first seemed such a far-fetched idea that one of the directors actually laughed in Seymour's face when told about it. The brainwave had come from Arthur Cox, Newcastle's manager from 1980 to 1984 and not someone with a reputation for such inspired thinking. But, belying his dour,

GENESIS

sergeant-majorish image, Cox enabled down-at-heel Newcastle to outflank the plutocrats of English football and acquire one of the biggest crowd-pullers of the game.

They were helped considerably in their machinations by the financial support of Scottish & Newcastle Breweries, the club's main sponsors. The arrangement was that the breweries would top up Keegan's wages in a separate deal for promotional work. And although both player and club tried hard to play down speculation that Keegan would be earning in excess of £3000 a week – a colossal sum in 1982 – there was little doubt that 'the greatest signing in Newcastle's history' would be the highest earner in the English game, for one season, at least.

In point of fact, Keegan's salary was a complicated business, geared to attendances and appearances. In approximate terms, it meant the club would pay him £1000 a week for playing football, while Scottish & Newcastle Breweries contributed a further £1500 for three nights' promotional work a week. The irony was, of course, that Keegan is a virtual teetotaller.

However, scruples apart, the deal must have been good enough for him not to have regretted giving up the £75,000 a year he had been receiving from Southampton.

Sensibly, Keegan's initial contract was restricted to a year. This was so that he could leave quickly if he felt he had made a mistake and so Newcastle could cut their losses if they found they had overstretched themselves financially. 'We've gambled, my God, we've gambled. This signing will either make us or break us at the bank,' one Newcastle director confessed nervously to John Gibson in the gents at the Gosforth Park Hotel following that tumultuous press conference to unveil Keegan.

There was no need to worry. As Gibson put it in his 1984 biography of the player, *Kevin Keegan – Portrait of a Superstar*: 'Bringing Keegan to Tyneside was like opening your own bank. The cash rolled in as supporters reacted to news which they found nothing less than sensational.' Several thousand people were locked out of St James' Park while a crowd of 36,000 craned eagerly inside to watch their new idol's Second Division debut for Newcastle against Queen's Park Rangers, one of the clubs fancied for promotion. Naturally enough, Keegan, a player with an uncanny sense of occasion, scored the winning goal – and at the famous Gallowgate End. 'I could feel the crowd sucking the ball into the net,' he said after running in among, and being feted by, the delirious fans behind the goal.

It was a defining moment in the story of Newcastle's revival. As Steve Wraith puts it, 'When Kevin pulled on that black and white shirt and scored against Queen's Park Rangers on his debut, it was the start of a great relationship. Nothing had ever happened like that, you know. He was probably the greatest player Newcastle United had had since Tony Green, Malcolm Macdonald and Terry Hibbitt in the Seventies. We hadn't exactly been overloaded with fantastic players. Before Kevin arrived, Imre Varadi and the up-and-coming Chris Waddle were the only two in the team who had any sparkle.' Wraith, twenty-six and the editor of one of Newcastle's most popular fanzines, the *No. 9*, is just about old enough to chronicle the period and assess its significance. But there's no doubting the impression the occasion made on him and thousands of supporters like him.

Keegan's debut was the start of a season that promised much, both on and off the field, but which served only to improve Newcastle's bank balance. While the average gate shot up to 24,510 – 7000 higher than the previous season – there was not enough class and experience in the team to respond consistently and effectively to the typically dynamic leadership of Keegan, who scored twenty-one goals in thirty-seven League games. Points were frittered away, and not even a powerful late surge could lift them higher than fifth place behind the promoted clubs, QPR, Wolverhampton Wanderers and Leicester.

This, too, despite the Pied Piper effect Keegan had had upon Newcastle. His decision to go to St James' Park encouraged other big names to follow. In no time at all he was rejoined by Terry McDermott and Mick Channon, two old mates from club and international football, and joined by David McCreery, the Northern Ireland and former Manchester United midfielder,

GENESIS

from American soccer. But Channon's loan deal did not work out, and not even McDermott and McCreery could provide enough of what was needed from the middle of the park.

No one was more aware of the team's deficiencies than Keegan, a man never satisfied with second-best. So, in a manoeuvre that was to be repeated when he became manager nine years later, he deliberately put the club under pressure to strengthen the side further. Having warned in an *Evening Chronicle* interview that he wanted to see Newcastle sign some players of real quality before committing himself to another one-year contract, he revealed to the *Sun* that the new deal would contain escape clauses enabling him to opt out at varying stages of the season if promotion became unlikely.

'I'm not holding a gun to their head, but I want to see some movement from the club,' he told the *Chronicle*. 'I want to play with a better all-round squad next season so that we can gain more success. It's as much for the benefit of the fans as for myself. They deserve so much after all this time. The boss and the chairman know exactly how I feel, so I'm not talking behind their back ... But at this stage of my career I don't want failure.'

However, Keegan's revelations in the *Sun*, for whom he has always written occasional columns, caused a sharp division of opinion among even the most loyal of Newcastle's fans. Coupled with the news that he had moved his family back to Hampshire, they made some supporters think the unthinkable and wonder whether he was fully committed to the cause. The majority, on the other hand, preferred to believe their hero was simply twisting the board's arm to get what the club needed after spending too much of the post-war period in the wilderness.

What followed, though clearly a response to Keegan's nagging, could hardly be classed as a wild spending spree. Martin Thomas, a goalkeeper who had been on loan, was signed permanently and two new full backs, Malcolm Brown and John Ryan, were brought in for the grand total of £325,000. Indeed, the biggest transfer news on Tyneside in the summer of 1983 was the sale of Imre Varadi, Keegan's partner in attack, for £150,000 to Sheffield Wednesday, one of Newcastle's rivals for promotion from the Second Division. Since Varadi had scored forty-two goals in two seasons following his transfer from Everton, it appeared a rash move.

The fee for the somewhat erratic striker could not have been put to better use, however. It enabled Newcastle to bring back that native son, Peter Beardsley, to St James' Park from his second spell in Canada with Vancouver Whitecaps. That a player of Beardsley's quality was twice forced to go abroad to find a club is quite incredible; but at least Newcastle, who had missed out on him in the first place, got it right in the end.

Beardsley, with his silky touch, quick thinking and fertile imagination, proved a much better partner for Keegan than Varadi, whose tearaway style had not gone down too well with a man used to having the ball played to feet. In fact, as soon as Beardsley was asked to start a game for the first time, against Portsmouth at home on 1 October 1983, Newcastle embarked on a searing run of six consecutive wins that carried them into second place.

But it was not just a Keegan and Beardsley show. Chris Waddle, like Beardsley then only twenty-two, suddenly began to fulfil his potential in the inspiring company of two such gifted team-mates. When you think about it now, it is hardly surprising that Newcastle went on to win promotion to the First Division – albeit only in third place behind Chelsea and Sheffield Wednesday – with three world-class footballers in attack.

However, just as the club and their supporters were beginning to close in on the prize and daydream about their prospects in the top flight, Keegan shocked them with one of his typically forthright and dramatic decisions. On St Valentine's Day in 1984 – his thirty-third birthday – he announced he would be quitting football at the end of that season. The timing of the announcement – in the latter stages of a tense promotion campaign – might have been questionable, but he was determined

GENESIS

to quash all the speculation there had been about the possibility of his joining another club.

'I've made up my mind to retire and nothing will change it,' said Keegan, who had revealed that losing out to Liverpool's gazelle-like defender Mark Lawrenson in a race for the ball had prompted the decision. 'I'm lucky to be able to quit while I believe I am still at the top. I want Newcastle's fans to realize that I won't be leaving them to play for another club. I'll kick the last competitive ball of my career in a Newcastle shirt. That's the highest possible tribute I can pay to a tremendous football public.'

And so it came to pass that the day arrived when, to much lamentation, this true messiah ascended into the heavens. By helicopter, actually, at the end of positively the last of several emotional farewells – a friendly against Liverpool, Keegan's old club, at St James' on 17 May 1984. The game ended as a 2–2 draw, but none of the 36,722 Geordies packed into the ground cared much about the result. Their only concern was to pay homage to the man who, by leadership and example, had revitalized the most important thing in most of their lives – Newcastle United Football Club.

But let a man who was there, Alan Oliver, chief sports writer for the *Evening Chronicle*, paint the picture. In his revealing and perceptive account of Keegan's fruitful association with Newcastle, *Geordie Messiah – The Keegan Years*, Oliver writes: 'If those previous laps of honour had been spontaneous demonstrations of emotion, what happened on the final whistle was pre-planned, stage-managed and, some might say, over the top.

'But football had never quite witnessed an exit like this. Keegan had arranged a party for family, friends and team-mates at the Gosforth Park Hotel that night, but before the drinks could flow it was time to bid farewell to his disciples. A helicopter hovered over the stadium as an emotional Keegan, now on his own, walked around the perimeter before hovering in front of the West Stand and picking out his wife and young children in the directors' box.

THE MAGNIFICENT OBSESSION

'Then the helicopter landed on the centre circle and, with the crowd not knowing whether to laugh, cry or cheer, he ran towards its door, turning once to wave a last goodbye. It must have been a strange sight watching thousands of hardened Geordies peering up to the heavens with their arms raised until the aircraft became a blip. But then for the last two years, Newcastle United had reached for the skies. At the time, no one would have guessed they would try and reach even higher under Kevin Keegan the manager.'

Maybe not, but most were acutely aware of the profound change Keegan had brought about in the psychology and attitude of the club during his short but successful time with them as a player. He had bullied and cajoled them into meeting the high standards he set for himself and he had taught them to think and behave like winners. In the process, of course, he endeared himself to fans for whom the well-being of Newcastle United was almost more important than life itself, and who had been starved of success for years.

'I was there that day,' says Labour councillor Terry Cooney, 'and there was a lot of tears and heavy hearts, I can tell you.' Cooney, whose support for the club goes back to the great FA Cup-winning side in the Fifties of Jackie Milburn, Joe Harvey, Frank Brennan and Bobby Mitchell, says of Keegan's first spell with Newcastle: 'That was the start, as far as I'm concerned.

'Because if you think about what happened, we didn't just have Keegan here, we had Beardsley and Waddle as well. I know he gave them both advice, particularly Waddle. Waddle had his moments when he wasn't doing everything he should have been doing on the field because of his social life off the field in those days, and Keegan made it clear to him he had to pull his socks up if he wanted to earn his living out of the game. Because of his coaching abilities, Keegan affected the players as well.'

Not to put too fine a point on it, Keegan was practically running the club as captain of the team. Although he may not have realized it at the time, he was going through a kind of crash course in management. In all respects he proved beyond doubt in his first spell at St James' that he had the strength of character and personality to dominate a situation and the charisma to lead and inspire others.

He also bonded with the fans in a way that guaranteed him a lifetime's acceptance as an honorary Geordie. The venom with which some Newcastle supporters reacted to the brave, seminal decision of the new England manager, Bobby Robson, to drop Keegan from the national squad in the autumn of 1982 is not to be applauded: spitting at anyone is bad enough, but even worse when the unfortunate recipient is one of your own, as Robson was and is. Nevertheless, the very fact that some were prepared to exceed the bounds of acceptable behaviour in Keegan's defence is proof of the fans' veneration of him as the natural heir to Hughie Gallacher, Jackie Milburn and Malcolm Macdonald, the three other deities in Newcastle's history.

Nor did he sully the relationship by joining another club. 'Newcastle supporters are peculiar people,' says John Gibson. 'If you desert the club, which is what it amounts to in their eyes if you leave to go elsewhere – like Chris Waddle, Paul Gascoigne or, the first time round, Peter Beardsley did – you are looked upon as something of a traitor. Waddle, certainly, has never been forgiven and gets stick whenever he plays up here as a result. That's because he was the first of the three young superstars to desert, in the eyes of the fans. So they have never forgiven him.

'Keegan, on the other hand, decided to retire. So that cemented the relationship between him and the fans. The only way you could go out the door and be accepted was the way Malcolm Macdonald went, i.e. forced out by Gordon Lee. Unless you were forced out, it was unforgivable if you left for a bigger club. You could grumble about Newcastle being unsuccessful, but you still weren't supposed to leave the club. The fans didn't, so the players weren't supposed to, either.

'The fact that Keegan didn't desert us, just went into retirement, enhanced his reputation on Tyneside. When he came back [as manager eight years later], that wonderful feeling was there because he was the guy who used to be with Newcastle and retired having achieved promotion for them. So when he walked back in, he was a hero.'

There was an awful lot of water to flow under the bridge before that happened, though. Eight years of it, in fact. Time enough for two World Cups, those of 1986 and 1990, in which England did unusually well under Bobby Robson, the man who had ended Keegan's international career so controversially. Time enough, too, for Keegan himself to have lost all contact with and all interest in the game. That clearly did not happen. In the event, it looked as though he had just been waiting for the right moment, and the right offer, to come back.

2

THE WILDERNESS YEARS

During Kevin Keegan's eight-year absence from St James' Park, Newcastle went absolutely nowhere. That is not strictly true. After getting back into the former First Division following Keegan's help as a player, they spent five rather undistinguished seasons there before slipping back into the Second Division. During that five-year spell between 1984 and 1989, only once did Newcastle finish anywhere near the pinnacle of English football – they finished eighth in the 1987–88 season, at the end of Willie McFaul's three-year spell in charge. McFaul, the former Newcastle goalkeeper, was the second of four managers who came and went at St James' Park during those wilderness years. The others, in order, were Jack Charlton, who promptly and typically walked out when the fans called for his resignation a year after he had arrived, the nomadic Jim Smith and the dapper little former Argentine international Ossie Ardiles.

Arthur Cox, who had had the bright idea of persuading Keegan to finish his playing career at Newcastle and actually took the club back up into the old First Division, did not hang around long at St James' Park after Keegan had departed. He resigned to become manager of Derby County, then in the Third Division. Terry McDermott left, too, as a pattern of departures began to establish itself. Worst of all, as far as the long-suffering fans were concerned, was the club's willingness to sell its best players, especially the local lads. Chris Waddle was the first to go. He joined Tottenham for £590,000 in 1985. Then Peter Beardsley went to Liverpool for £1.9 million in 1987. The final straw came when Paul Gascoigne, arguably the finest talent ever unearthed on Tyneside, was sold to Tottenham Hotspur in 1988 for £2 million.

'In the period between Keegan playing and managing,' says John Gibson, 'we saw a situation where the club, instead of building on the success that Keegan the player had achieved, collapsed. Before the next season started, Arthur Cox, who had masterminded his signing, quit because Newcastle United would not give him the money to buy the players he wanted for the top division. Arthur went off to manage Derby, two divisions down. Terry McDermott never kicked another ball for Newcastle and then, all of a sudden, they sell Waddle, they sell Beardsley and they sell Gascoigne. So Newcastle were looked upon as a selling club. What was unforgivable about it was that they had three Geordie superstars who were allowed to leave their home town. Sometimes up here you had the feeling you couldn't hold on to cockneys because they wanted to go back down to the Smoke; but when you couldn't hold on to your own, you knew the club was definitely going nowhere.'

The board may have been happy to rake in £4.5 million from the sale of those three players in as many years, but the fans, increasingly discontented at not having won a major domestic trophy since the three FA Cups in the 1950s, correctly interpreted the club's transfer policy as a complete lack of ambition. Director Stan Seymour Jnr, son of Newcastle's famously powerful former manager and director, virtually spelled it out once when comparing his club with Liverpool. 'Well, of course, we'll never be like them,' he said. 'We'll never be as good as them.'

That damning remark was recalled by Bob Cass of the *Mail on Sunday*, who has covered the football of his native North East since the 1960s. 'They talk about Newcastle being a sleeping giant,' says Cass, 'but it was more comatose than asleep: there wasn't anything happening there. You could see where football was going, but not Newcastle.' Cass decided to do something about it. Short of a piece for a sports supplement his newspaper was producing at the time, he thought it might be a good idea to go and interview a wealthy property developer who was said to be willing to put money into the club. That man was a certain John Hall.

'It was a situation that had been boiling up at Newcastle,' Cass recalls. 'In my position, you want all the North East clubs to do well; and I felt Newcastle weren't going to get anywhere with the kind of nepotism that had existed there for years, with shares being handed down from generation to generation and not a lot of money being put into the club. To be fair, Newcastle had won three cups in the 1950s when the old board was in charge; but it's now over seventy years since they won the title. People have been born, grown up and died without seeing Newcastle win the League Championship. You'd have to be an octogenarian to have been alive when Newcastle last won the title. And I felt, Christ, this is always going to be the case. Even so, I wouldn't go so far as to call it a crusade – all I was going to do was speak to John Hall for a piece I was writing.

'There had been speculation linking this property developer, whom I had never met in my life before, with putting money into the club. So I arranged to go and see him and went to where they were building the Metro Centre. It had been opened, but they were still building there and had kind of prefabricated offices on the site. John and I had a talk in one of the offices about the Newcastle situation, but he virtually said, "Why do I want to get involved in all that?" So I said, "Because it needs somebody like you."

'Just before we met, Tom Cowie had taken over at Sunderland, and although I wasn't instrumental in that, I knew the Tom Cowie aides who'd been supporting him in his takeover. So with that sort of fresh in my mind, I said, "It needs somebody like you to get involved. You are a Newcastle supporter, you were brought up as a Newcastle supporter. Look, the place is going nowhere. It needs your kind of vision and clout to pull it out of the shit." He still wasn't very keen, but I urged him to just give it a try. In the end, he said, "All right, I'll act as a catalyst." He felt the club should belong to the supporters, and he said he would make an approach to the board and ask if there was any way he could help.

'By the time we finished the interview, he had agreed to make approaches but he wasn't going to go in there and put loads of cash in – that was never his intention at the start. What he was going to do was get involved, see if there was anything he could do and offer any expert help that he felt he could in business terms. In the piece I wrote about him he talked about the Metro Centre regenerating the economy of the area and asked how much a part of the regeneration a successful football club would be. He felt it was important in that context.'

Sir John verifies every detail of Cass's version of that fateful meeting, and then some. Retracing the steps that led him into the chairmanship of Newcastle, he says, 'People had asked me to get involved in the club, but I'd refused because I had too much on. I was building the Metro Centre and I was developing the business [Cameron Hall Developments], so that was a job in itself. In the end, it was Bob Cass of the *Mail on Sunday* who actually got me involved. I didn't know Bob personally then, but I knew of him because he and John Gibson used to do the talk-ins with the fans around the pubs where they were asking when somebody was going to do something about Newcastle United.

'Because of the Metro Centre and the profile I had in the area, they seemed to home in on me for help. Bob came to see me two or three times, I think, but I told him I wasn't interested. Then, about the third time he came, I'd had one of those weeks. It was a Friday afternoon, I remember, and it was raining. We met in the Portakabins at the Metro Centre and he said, "You've got to do something, John." Now I don't normally have a drink at work, and I'm not a spirits man, but Bob and I saw off a bottle of whisky we kept in the office for entertaining guests. It had been a bad week, and sometimes you just do something to get away from it all. Not surprisingly, perhaps, I mellowed and said, "OK, Bob, I'll start it off by putting half a million pounds on the table." I told him I didn't want the club for myself: I wanted it for the fans, because I felt it was a fans' club.'

Unfortunately, the Newcastle board wanted nothing to do with Hall, his entrepreneurial money, his business expertise or his fancy democratic ideas. So far as they were concerned, he looked more like a threat to their cosy existence than a knight in shining armour. 'What happened when he offered his help,' says Cass, 'is that they told him to piss off. They said thank you very much, but no thanks. Well, that got his back up a bit and he took them on eventually. There was only one winner once he wanted to get his teeth into it. He was never going to lose: this fellow does not lose. John's a reasonable man, but he's a ruthless bugger when people start rubbing him up the wrong way.'

What followed was a long and bitter battle for control of Newcastle United. Hall and his merry men won it by mounting a massive, all-out campaign to gain a controlling interest in the club and, crucially, backing it up with the support of the *Evening Chronicle*. 'Because John felt that without a daily platform to have his say the campaign wouldn't work, the *Evening Chronicle* was approached,' recalls John Gibson. 'Once the paper decided to make a stand, I was delegated to be the man. And, I must say, from the paper's point of view it was a very brave stand to make, because this guy didn't even have one share. It was also made quite apparent very early on by the existing board of directors that, if they won, neither myself nor the *Chronicle* would be welcome at St James' Park again.'

Calling themselves the Magpie Group, the rebels went round buying up shares wherever they could find them and persuade the owners to sell, sometimes paying as much as £7000 per share. It was not as easy as it sounds, if only because the shares had become widely dispersed over the years and took some finding in many cases. 'It was a great piece of detective work to locate all the shares,' points out Bob Cass. 'They had to track them down all over the world. It became a big exercise, buying up shares here, buying up shares there and offering fortunes for them. Families who'd had their shares for years and said they would never, ever sell to the Magpie Group were suddenly cashing in. There were big supporters of the club who said there was no way they were getting involved; but suddenly I'd get a call at night and be told, "So-and-so's selling out!" And I'd say, "You're joking!" So, slowly but surely, John got into a position where the others had to capitulate.

'I was never a member of the Magpie Group myself, but what we used to do was go round working-men's clubs explaining the situation to supporters. I would chair the question-and-answer sessions, and that kind of thing. It was a political campaign, in effect: it was like being on the hustings. I was very happy because I'd managed to get a good piece out of it and, at the same time, started off something that was very dear to me. There were tremendous hiccups at the start, and you wondered what was going to happen, but you felt it was beginning to go in the right direction.'

As Cass indicates, it was hardly a smooth ride. Hall's enduring reluctance to get involved nearly saw him walk away from the whole business at least once. Not only that, but the old-school board, led by chairman Gordon McKeag, offered stiffer resistance than might have been expected. McKeag, a local solicitor, had been a director of the club for more than fifteen years and was fighting for his heritage. He was one of the two sons of Alderman William McKeag, a former chairman of Newcastle United and a powerful figure in the Tyneside area.

Bob Cass likens William McKeag to Bob Lord, the intimidating baron of Burnley in the 1960s and 1970s. 'These fellows never put a shilling into their clubs, but were regarded with tremendous awe by everybody,' he says, quite rightly. That was the thing about the old board: in common with the directors of most other English professional clubs at the time, they wanted the privilege and prestige that came with the position but not the financial responsibility. In other words, they were reluctant to invest any of their own money in the club. As Cass recalls, 'There was a brilliant surgeon, Fenton Braithwaite, on the board at one

THE WILDERNESS YEARS

time. He owned half the Golden Mile at Blackpool and was an exceedingly rich man. It wasn't that there wasn't any money there: they just didn't put their hands in their pockets to do anything about it.'

Sir John Hall, too, is able to put that difficult situation in perspective now. 'I don't think Newcastle was any different to football in general at the time,' he says. 'If you look at the origins of clubs like ours, who are over a hundred years old, they were built by entrepreneurs like myself who formed the football club, ran the football club, put money in and shared in the passion and the feeling. Then, as those men died, the shares became dissipated among their families and nobody had absolute control. In some cases, too, the wealth of some of those families diminished, so there wasn't the will or the wealth to do anything. You had reached a situation where nobody was willing to invest the vast sums required to compete at the highest level of the game.

'Newcastle were lucky because we generate our own kids in this area. The North East has always been the place for finding talent, and still is today. We had the Waddles, the Beardsleys and the Gascoignes, but we let them go. So, in a sense, we sold the equity to pay off the debt. Players come and go with alarming regularity in football, but if you are selling off your best players to pay off debts you are in trouble, because your equity's gone. Newcastle reached the point, after Gascoigne went, when there wasn't any equity left. So the club wasn't going anywhere: it was in a vacuum. Unless there was an injection of vast sums of money, Newcastle would never be able to compete with the leading clubs in the country in a changing League scenario.'

The majority of the poor, long-suffering supporters are not quite so forgiving about that inglorious chapter in the club's history. Taken for granted and treated with disdain – as until quite recently seemed the fashion in English football in general – the people who had supplied the bulk of the club's income prior to sponsorship and mega-TV deals creating real wealth could only burn helplessly with anger and frustration. They watched their beloved club stagnate and did not fully understand why. 'The only regret I had about Kevin Keegan's time as a Newcastle player,' said Steve Wraith, 'was that he didn't stay for one more season and play in the First Division with Beardsley and Waddle. Maybe things might have been a little bit different if he had.

'But I don't suppose they would, because the board we had in at the time seemed to be intent on just one thing and that was raking in money. Not putting the money back into the club, not investing it. It was only when the Hillsborough disaster occurred [in 1989] that Newcastle United actually forced themselves to spend some money on improving their ground. I'm sure everyone remembers the Bradford fire in 1985 . . . Well, Newcastle United had a stand – the old West Stand – which could equally well have gone up in the same kind of manner as the one at Bradford.

'We look at all the developments which have made St James' a bastion of invincibility over the last few years, but when plans were submitted in the sixties for the Leazes' development everyone was expecting great things. That should have been done years ago. We shouldn't have been sitting in the late eighties and early nineties watching a stand go up. Newcastle were a tight-fisted club until the Magpie Group came into the equation during the 1988–89 season. John Hall himself has got one aim: to make money. But you can't take anything away from him. He's been a very successful businessman and he's ploughed his money into the club. Those new stands wouldn't be there for him and we wouldn't have had the money to attract somebody like Kevin Keegan.'

Fortunately for Newcastle and all who worship the club, Hall triumphed eventually after a number of false starts in what gradually became a bid to gain absolute control. Originally, as we have heard, he was intent on spreading ownership of the club among the fans, a concept he now regards as naive. 'When I met some of the Newcastle directors,' he says, 'they made it clear they didn't want what I was offering. So my son, Douglas, said, "Give me £1 million, dad, and I'll go and buy the shares." But I wanted to be ever so democratic and fair:

THE WILDERNESS YEARS

I didn't really want the club for myself, to be honest. So I said, "No, I'll get blasted, Douglas." But he was right and I was wrong. We should have done what he suggested. Two or three years later, we had spent £4 million buying shares and had only forty per cent of them.'

That qualified success left the Halls in a very invidious position. They had become the possessors of Newcastle's major shareholding, but still did not have overall control of a club with debts of about £6.5 million and a stadium urgently in need of redevelopment following the Taylor Report, which had recommended the wholesale refurbishment of Britain's football grounds in response to the Hillsborough disaster of 1989. 'They had to invite me on to the board because I was the biggest shareholder,' says Sir John, 'but it wasn't an easy time. I must admit Gordon [McKeag] marshalled his defences well. He had his ideas and I had mine, and all I wanted was the democratization of the club. The board then had a share issue, but the fans didn't take it up. The share issue wasn't for the purposes I wanted: it was necessary to get money in to save the club. Whether the fans were still suspicious of the old board or not, I don't know, but it was a flop.

'So, having set out to have a share issue and seen it fail, I felt I'd done everything I wanted to. Even though we were in for £4 million, I didn't want to own the club. So I stepped aside and gave the power of my shares to George Forbes, another of the directors, and told him to get on and run the club because I didn't want to know. George loved Newcastle so much he wanted to give up his job and become chairman full-time, and I thought I was finished with Newcastle United at that point.'

Sir John underlined his lack of desire to rule the roost at St James' Park by going on a round-the-world holiday. It was a celebration of Thomas Cook's 150th anniversary, and it took Sir John and Lady Mae Hall to Hong Kong, among many other exotic places. Then, all of a sudden, the outside world intruded. 'I got a telephone call from Douglas,' recalls Sir John. 'He'd tracked me down in Hong Kong, and said the Newcastle board needed £1 million. The other directors wouldn't put their money in unless we put ours in, apparently. But I wasn't keen on the idea. I told Douglas to let it go, not to get involved any more. I said your first loss is always your cheapest: it's going to cost us £4 million, but we can carry it. Finally, I suggested we should leave it until I got back in a fortnight's time. To which he replied, "Dad, you've got two hours. The bank will pull the plug if it's not sorted out, and you can't let the club go."'

Hall's reluctant reaction to his son's chivvying was to authorize a payment of £680,000 to save Newcastle from bankruptcy. 'It was the most expensive telephone call of my life,' he recalls. What had happened was that the board, deeply in hock to the bank, had failed to honour an undertaking not to buy players with an additional £1 million overdraft (on top of the existing £4 million). They had paid £300,000 of it to Leicester City for striker David Kelly, so the bank asked for their money back. Such irresponsible behaviour by Newcastle infuriated Hall, and convinced him there was nothing else to do but take complete charge of the club.

'When I came back from holiday I was angry and determined to protect the cash we'd put into the club. I found they'd got the budget figures wrong and gone out and bought a player. To be fair, I'd told them before I left that if they ever needed any more money from us, then I'd have to look at the situation again to protect our financial interest. So I went and saw George (Forbes) and said, "I'm sorry, but you haven't done what you said you would, and you've got to leave the chair." Sadly, he became a bitter enemy of mine, as I went back on the board. They gave me the tousing of my life, but at the end of the day people were realizing there was nowhere else to go.'

The final, desperate hope of the *ancien régime* was that Sir John, as he had become in 1991, would, in his own words, 'go upside down', when given full responsibility for running Newcastle United. Some hope! Conscious of his own lack of expertise in this area, he took the logical business step of bringing in someone who had plenty. That aide was Freddie

THE WILDERNESS YEARS

Fletcher, a little Scotsman who was to play a major and crucial role in the regeneration of Newcastle. A former director of the Scottish club Greenock Morton, Fletcher had found fame as the chief executive of Glasgow Rangers during Graeme Souness' controversial reign as manager in the late 1980s. He had helped Souness carry out a major overhaul of the playing staff and assisted in the transformation of Ibrox into one of the finest modern stadiums in Britain. He was perfect for the job at St James' Park, not only because of that impressive c.v. but also because he was already familiar with the situation there. A close friend of David Stephenson, the then managing director of Scottish & Newcastle Breweries, Fletcher had acted as an adviser to the Magpie Group.

Fletcher soon joined forces at St James' Park with Douglas, Sir John's son, and Freddie Shepherd, to form a powerful triumvirate on the board. Douglas, who has been running his father's property developing company, Cameron Hall, since Sir John decided to call it a day in 1993 at the age of sixty, is regarded as an even tougher businessman than his old man. The evidence certainly shows that Douglas has played almost as big a part as Sir John in the re-establishment of their beloved Newcastle United as one of the major clubs in the land. As for Shepherd, he was one of the substantial, long-standing shareholders who helped to tip the balance in favour of the Halls during the takeover war. Wealthy in his own right, as the owner of an offshore services company on the Tyne, Shepherd was rewarded for his support of the football club by being made vice-chairman. This, in effect, was the small, tightly-knitted group who masterminded the transformation of Newcastle United.

Sir John himself refused to bear any grudges at the end of what had been a particularly bitter battle for control of the club. He knew that basically the old directors cared as much about Newcastle United as anyone – the essential difference between him and them was that he was prepared to back his support with hard cash. Gordon McKeag certainly remains a figure of some distinction. Sir John could not hide his respect for the man, nor could Bob Cass. 'I felt sorry for Gordon,' admits Cass. 'Of all the chairmen Newcastle had before Sir John, I think he was the most forward-looking. What Gordon should have done is welcomed John in from the start, and they would have avoided all the blood-letting. If there had been some cooperation, all the nastiness and bitterness might not have happened. It was a really bitter fight to get those shares.

'It finished up with Gordon and his group being ostracized. He's allowed into the club now, but never into the boardroom. He was given an honorary title that allowed him to continue as president of the Football League, because you are supposed to be the director of a club to hold that position [McKeag, having become president in January 1992, was made independent chairman of the Football League's shadow board of directors during the restructuring of English football caused by the formation of the Premier League later that same year]. He's a nice man and I've got a lot of time for him, but he wasn't in a position to do for Newcastle what John Hall did. If they'd got together, who knows?'

There is no doubt that McKeag's vast experience of football administration would have been useful to the Halls. But what Newcastle needed more than anything at that point in its history was drive, vision and lots of money. Sir John Hall could supply all of those things in abundance. In the 1997 *Sunday Times* rankings of Britain's hundred wealthiest people, he was equal eighteenth, with a personal fortune estimated at £220 million. Most of it was garnered from the building of the Metro Centre, Europe's first and biggest indoor shopping mall, which was opened at Gateshead in two stages, one in 1984 and the other in 1986.

That massive £250 million project was the making of Hall and his property company, Cameron Hall Developments. He deserved every penny he got when he subsequently sold out to the Church Commissioners, because he had given ten years of his life to realizing an idea that was ahead of its time. He had been to America to study the out-of-town shopping centres that were becoming popular there, and had possessed the determination,

THE WILDERNESS YEARS

nerve and self-belief to push through a development that most other people dismissed as insane. For one thing, the site itself consisted of the old settling tanks for the local power station. In Sir John's own words, 'It was a tip. It was floating on water. They used to pump the water and the ash into ponds. The water would drain off, then they'd take out the ash and sell it. When I went out and got options on the land from five owners, they thought I was quaint.'

What the site had going for it was designation as one of the enterprise zones Thatcher's Government had copied from America, where Hall, a self-confessed admirer of the Iron Lady and her doctrine of free enterprise, had seen how they manipulated the tax system to get development off the ground in run-down areas. Apart from the financial incentives implicit in such zones, the local authority was allowed to write the rules. 'So it gave us freedom from the planning regimes,' says Sir John (who, interestingly, also counts Mao Tse-tung and his belief in constant revolution among his greatest influences). But there was still the hard slog ahead of persuading sceptical retailers to take space in this entirely new shopping concept. Not until he made the breakthrough with Marks & Spencer could Hall be sure the whole thing would work.

This, then, was the man Newcastle United were getting as their new leader: tough, determined, resilient, ambitious, far-sighted and wealthy. Just about perfect for the job of reviving the club, in fact. Better still, he was a true Newcastle fan. Born in Ashington, the mining town north of Newcastle famous for producing the Milburn and Charlton footballing dynasties (he went to the same school as Bobby Charlton), Hall had been brought up by his miner father in the strict family tradition of worshipping the team in black and white stripes. He worked down the pit himself for fourteen years as a mining surveyor, then he qualified as a chartered surveyor, came up top and began the dabbling in property which eventually made him a multi-millionaire.

Even so, he was still just one Newcastle fan among many

when the call came to get the club out of trouble. 'I remember standing on the terraces,' he says, launching into a misty-eyed recollection of how it used to be. 'I can tell you now, there's no way I could have imagined being up in the directors' box. I used to stand there in awe of the place. Every bloke from Ashington supported Newcastle. My father took me and his father took him, so it's gone through generations. We stood on the terraces in the rain in the days when they used to pee down your back. You have these great memories of things in life, and that was one of them – standing on the popular side with the pie shop there. There was a plank of wood on the fence, and if you got there early your dad would put you on the plank. If you didn't, you were rolled over to the front. There were 60,000 crowds then – 50,000-odd regular.

'I was still on the terraces when I was approached by Bob Cass to do something about Newcastle. I used to stand in different parts of the ground then – usually the posher end rather than the popular end – but still on the terraces.' Then comes a truly awful confession for a Newcastle fan to make: 'I used to live in Sunderland,' confides Sir John, 'so I would go to Sunderland one week and Newcastle the next. I had a season ticket at Sunderland, but I don't think I had one for Newcastle.'

He changed his place of abode rather spectacularly once he had sold the Metro Centre to the Church Commissioners for an enormous amount of money. In his own words, 'Afterwards, I went to America again and saw a scheme which consisted of a golf course with a business park and houses round it. I thought it was a good idea, and was pleased on my return to be told by an architect that the Wynyard Hall Estate was up for sale. It had been up for sale for two years. As soon as I came through the gates and saw it – all 5,500 acres of it – I knew it was ideal.'

The Durham estate, for centuries the home of the Marquess of Londonderry, was exactly what Sir John wanted for his next commercial venture. It cost him only £5 million to buy, though he has since spent as much again on bringing it up to scratch. Even at £10 million, it was a wonderfully cheap investment. Having spent two and a half years obtaining planning permission from five separate authorities, he is now in a position to build two or three golf courses surrounded by two hotels, 1000 upmarket houses and four million square feet of business park. 'The houses are going well and we are just about to open up the business park,' he reported in August 1997. 'It's the North East's next growth point.'

It is also his home. He and Lady Mae live in the Palladian mansion the Londonderrys used to regard as their aristocratic inheritance. It costs a fortune to keep up, he says: £250,000 a year to be precise. But the estate serves another useful purpose in providing suitably luxurious and protected accommodation for the more celebrated and expensive members of the Newcastle United staff. Kevin Keegan made his home there, and so has Alan Shearer. But we run ahead of ourselves – at this point in the story, neither Keegan nor Shearer figured very prominently as far as Sir John was concerned.

Hall was quite happy to stick with Ossie Ardiles as manager because he and Lady Mae had developed a strong personal relationship with the former Argentine international and his wife. After serving a three-year apprenticeship at Swindon, Ardiles had been taken on at Newcastle in 1991 as successor to the much-travelled, hard-working Jim Smith. But, under Ardiles, whose commitment to attacking football was so complete that it made Keegan's own adventurous play look positively cautious, Newcastle were leaking goals at an alarming rate. So much so that Douglas Hall felt it necessary to ring his father and demand the dismissal of a manager who seemed incapable of pulling the club out of its headlong dive towards the former Third Division, depths to which Newcastle had never before plunged in their history. As a result of a second decisive intervention by Hall Jnr, this tale was about to be given another twist.

3

THE SECOND COMING

Saint Kevin's reincarnation as manager of Newcastle in 1992 was even more amazing, if such a thing were possible, than his arrival there as a player ten years earlier. Consider the facts: in 1982 Keegan had been an active footballer of thirty-one, still very close to the height of his powers. His choice of the under-achieving Tyneside club as the final stop in his long and distinguished career was a big surprise, but there was never any question about his ability to deliver the goods. However, when it was announced a decade later that Keegan would be taking over as manager at St James' from the respected Ossie Ardiles, eyebrows throughout English football went into lift-off.

With good reason. After all, Keegan not only had no coaching qualifications or managerial experience, but also had been out of the game and out of the country for all of eight years – practically a generation in terms of the short career span of a footballer. While many of his former Liverpool, Southampton, Newcastle and England contemporaries, such as John Toshack, Glenn Hoddle, Emlyn Hughes, Ray Clemence, Ray Wilkins, Peter Shilton and Glenn Roeder, were launching their managerial careers and learning the ropes with varying degrees of success, Keegan appeared to be doing nothing more career-advancing or relevant than bringing down his golf handicap to a single figure by dint of constant practice on the lush golf courses of southern Spain.

As with everything else he has ever done in life, Keegan put his heart and soul into improving himself as a golfer. Living as he did in a luxurious residence overlooking the seventh green at the Rio Real club a few miles east of Marbella, there was ample opportunity to hone his natural ball skills. Those daily rounds of his soon became a byword among the Spanish caddies for dedication, fanaticism even. Friends who came out from England to play a round with him certainly noticed how focused on the game he had become. Derek Pavis, the chairman of Notts County, was one. 'Kevin puts as much into his golf as he put into his football,' observed Pavis. 'He wanted to win and to perfect his game in doing so. I enjoyed our games together, but there was only one winner, and that was Kevin.'

Even the professionals were struck by the standard Keegan had achieved. Ian Woosnam, the 1991 US Masters champion and British Ryder Cup player, was moved to comment admiringly after dropping in at Marbella between international tournaments. 'Kevin's a first-class golfer, that's for sure,' said 'Woosie'. 'He works very hard to improve his game. If he hadn't been a brilliant footballer, then he might have done well in golf. He works so hard.' Even in adversity, that was true. Norman Fox, the *Independent on Sunday* sports writer, recalls the shock of coming across a sweaty Keegan trying to unearth his ball from an impossibly tangled thicket while Fox was covering a pro-am tournament at Moor Park. 'I could do without this pressure,' joked Keegan, unconvincingly. 'I should have stuck to football!'

But it was precisely to get away from the grinding demands of football they had all endured for so long that Keegan took his wife, Jean, and their two young daughters, Laura Jane and Sarah, to live in Marbella. As many other British ex-pats have discovered, though, even a lotus life in the sun can begin to pall after a while. It must have been especially hard for such a dedicated football man and restless spirit as Keegan to cut himself off from the game for so long. As my own former *Sunday Telegraph* colleague, John Moynihan, observed perceptively in his biography of the man, *Kevin Keegan – Black and White*, 'Living in hot countries can have a marked effect on expatriates like Keegan, and the desire to pack in the good life on the Costa del Sol would show itself from time to time through the odd outburst in the national press.'

Even then, with his obvious eagerness to become involved

in football once more increasing by the minute, few imagined Keegan would return as a manager. Had he not gone on the record more than once indicating his unwillingness – determination even – not to expose himself to the risks of management? 'It takes a certain type to be a manager,' he once said while still in Spain. 'It's foolish to think that because you're a better than average player, you are going to make a good manager. I'm not scared of failure, but I would sooner not do it than fail.' So, the natural assumption was that, if he did come back, it would be as a football pundit on television, a role in which he had displayed immense promise already.

Indeed, as he and his family prepared to leave Spain in 1990 and return to their other palatial home at Romsey, near Southampton, even Keegan was thinking about a career in the media. 'I hadn't thought about managing a club when we packed up and came home,' he later recalled. 'It was the last thing on my mind. My future seemed to lie with doing commentaries on radio and television. We would make our farm in Hampshire our base, breeding horses, enjoying life without being involved in the real game.' However, on 5 February 1992, there was Keegan being unveiled as Newcastle's new manager at yet another dramatic and tumultuous press conference at the Gosforth Park Hotel.

It was an astonishing U-turn which he explained at the time simply by saying, with that infallible PR touch of his, that he would have returned as a manager for no other club than Newcastle. But if Keegan's explanation was less than completely satisfying, there was no shortage of opinions from other people about the reasons for such a monumental change of mind. Derek Pavis, for instance, believed Keegan's long-term aim was to establish himself as a candidate for the England manager's job. 'Pure and simple, Kevin wanted to be manager of England,' he insisted. 'And the only way he could get it was to become a club manager, to allow himself four or five years in the front line.' There was certainly circumstantial evidence to support this theory in that during his Spanish exile Keegan had stated in print he wanted Bobby Robson's job. By February

1992, however, Robson had moved on to PSV Eindhoven and greater glory and Graham Taylor, his successor with England, had yet to reveal his shortcomings for the first time at the finals of the European Championship in Sweden later that year.

Others see Keegan's return to Newcastle as something that just happened because of a combination of circumstances. 'I think he was beginning to get bored with the golf abroad,' says John Gibson. 'If you've been prominent in football, you develop a need for the limelight; and I think, for a long time, Kevin revelled in it. Basically, it was just a question of being offered the right job at the right time.' It was the right time, argues the knowledgeable local newspaperman, because Keegan was in the process of being drawn back towards English football again and the right job because he would be returning as a hero to a well-supported club that had just acquired – through the addition to the board of Sir John Hall and his son Douglas – the administrative and financial capacity to pull out of the serious decline it had suffered since Keegan's own theatrical and lamented departure eight years earlier.

'He's a very clever boy, Keegan,' adds Gibson. 'He chose Newcastle both times, as a player and as a manager, because they were a true sleeping giant. If he'd gone to manage Liverpool, say, or Manchester United and they'd won the League title, so what? At Liverpool, everybody – Bill Shankly, Bob Paisley, Joe Fagan, Kenny Dalglish – won it. And Kevin knew he wouldn't be remembered for winning the championship somewhere where it was regularly won. He saw the potential in winning it with Newcastle United because they were as big a club, had as big a support, had as big a history as the Liverpools and Man Uniteds. Everybody thought he was a fool to go back to St James', but he was a very shrewd boy in making that choice. Newcastle might not have been in the top flight when he returned, but he knew they had the capacity – and the financial clout of the Halls – to get there.'

Then there was the question of the enduring mutual admiration between Keegan and the Newcastle supporters, a factor that has to be put somewhere near the top of the list of reasons

THE SECOND COMING

for his return. 'When Kevin left Newcastle,' continues Gibson, 'he said he wished he'd played there early in his career because the supporters were fantastic. They were fantastic because they were devoid of success and they suddenly saw Keegan and took him to their hearts. They took him to their hearts more than Manchester United and Liverpool supporters would a new player, because they've seen all the great stars at Old Trafford and Anfield. And Kevin knew if he was ever going to be a manager the place to build his reputation – with that kind of fan worship waiting for him – was Newcastle.'

If Keegan's decision to return to English football as manager of Newcastle was surprising, it was no more so than the club's choice of him for the job. It is difficult now, given the spectacular impact Keegan made as a manager, to imagine the enormity of the gamble Newcastle took in appointing him; but a gamble it certainly was. As has been pointed out already, he had the worst possible credentials if experience and logic were to count for anything in the selection process. All he had going for him was his increasingly distant reputation as a fine footballer and an engaging personality. By rights, the new Newcastle board should have gone for a seasoned manager in their efforts to pull the club out of its nosedive towards the old Third Division. But, for some reason – fate perhaps – they chose to respond to the suggestion by chief executive Freddie Fletcher that Keegan was the man who could revitalize the team.

'The staggering thing for me,' confesses John Gibson, 'is that the Halls ever thought of Kevin Keegan as manager. The club was in the doldrums and they needed a lift – a big lift – yet they didn't go for an established manager. They went for a man who was a big name in Newcastle, but he'd been out of the country, never mind football, for eight years. So he didn't know the current scene at all. But they knew what he'd done as a player and they knew they would get an immediate lift from the fans if they appointed him. They did something similar, incidentally, with Rob Andrew when they went into rugby. I find the decision to appoint Keegan as staggering as his to accept the job, but it turned out to be inspired.'

THE MAGNIFICENT OBSESSION

The unexpected identity of Newcastle's new manager was only half of a truly bizarre story, for the Hall faction pushed the appointment through without the knowledge or permission of the rest of the board. It was at a time when Sir John and Douglas did not yet have complete control, so they kept their plans secret from the other directors. Freddie Shepherd and Freddie Fletcher were the only other board members who knew what was going on, and that was enough. With Keegan already in town ready to be wheeled out at a morning press conference, Fletcher dashed round to the home of Ardiles, the incumbent and unsuspecting Newcastle manager, to sack him at 7.30 a.m. – only a couple of hours before the former Argentine international's successor was due to be announced. In other words, everyone was presented with a *fait accompli*.

Even Sir John was a bit of an onlooker as events unfolded. As John Gibson explains: 'John had got very close socially to Ossie, who was and is an absolute gentleman. Ossie's wife, Lady Mae and Sir John often had dinner together down at Wynyard Hall. John loved him, but Douglas is very hard-headed and a very shrewd businessman. And, when the results continued to go badly, he said, "That [his parents' friendship with the Ardileses] doesn't matter. This man has got to go!" It would be wrong to say it was all done behind John's back, but it was certainly done without his knowledge. John was mortified when he heard – not because he thought it was the wrong decision for Newcastle United, but because he loved the little man so dearly. So it was a real *coup d'état* on everybody, really, when Keegan first came.'

Even five years later, with all the excitement and pleasure of the Keegan era in between, it was clear that Sir John still felt the pain of the Ardiles dismissal. Those who reject him as a hard-boiled, insensitive character would do well to listen to his account of the managerial change-over at St James' Park in 1992. It might alter a few perceptions of him. 'I liked Ossie a lot – a hell of a lot,' admits Hall. 'We were personal friends. Not only that, but the club needed continuity. So when we got beaten 5–2 at Oxford on 1 February 1992, I called him in and asked whether he thought he could get through with the team he'd got. He said he needed to strengthen the side, but I told him he had to sell players to bankroll us because the club didn't have any cash. He said he knew who he would sell and mentioned two players. So I said OK, and left him with Douglas.

'It was the Monday morning after the match, and Mae and I were leaving at lunchtime for a dinner in London. We were actually down there getting changed – Mae's putting her dress on, you know, the jewellery, etc. – when the phone rang at seven o'clock that night. It was Douglas, and he said, "He's got to go!" I said, "Who are you talking about?" and he replied, "Ossie." I said, "What do you mean? What do you mean? You can't do that!" But Douglas insisted Ossie had lost his way and we needed to make a change. I said, "Don't be so daft. What's the matter with the lad?" He said Ossie had gone out to sell players and found he couldn't. We were in a no-win situation because I hadn't been present at the meeting. My wife was nearly in tears because we were very good friends with them, and this was something we weren't used to doing. People think I'm a hard man, but I've never been ruthless in that sense. I have had to do hard things, but not when they're personal friends. It's difficult.'

Quite obviously, Douglas Hall and the two Freddies had already lined up Keegan as Ardiles' successor when Douglas rang his father in London that night. Having called for Ardiles' dismissal, Hall Jnr said a meeting had been arranged with Keegan the following morning at a hotel on Park Lane and asked Sir John to attend it. 'They had made their decision, Freddie [Fletcher] and Douglas,' recalls Hall Snr. 'They said it was the best thing for the club if Ossie were to go. It was difficult for me and my wife to take in. We couldn't understand it.'

Despite the shock and embarrassment of Ardiles' sudden axing, Sir John had enough faith in the judgement of his son and Freddie Fletcher to go along with the decision to bring in a new manager. He went to the pow-wow on Park Lane and met Keegan for the first time. 'I didn't know Kevin, but Freddie knew him from the two years he was with Newcastle as a player and doing things for the brewery. Freddie had met him through his own contacts with the brewery. When I made the point that Kevin had been out of the game for years, Freddie said, "The fans love him. He'll do it!" So the inspiration for the appointment came from Freddie Fletcher and Douglas Hall. You've got to give them credit for that, because it was an inspired appointment.

'There was only one way to go with it, because we were in relegation trouble: we were practically down in the Third Division. I told Kevin that was the scenario at the club and I think we said my wife and I were prepared to put in half a million pounds for players. I think he must have wondered what he was coming into. We weren't in charge at that time: we only had forty per cent of the shares. It was the old board, with myself as chairman, so we were not in absolute control. The old board could have outvoted us, but I think they took the attitude, "Let them hang themselves. They'll not make it work." Anyway, I left Freddie and Douglas to talk terms with Kevin. They agreed, he came and that was the start of the Keegan era. But it was the last throw of the dice in many, many ways.'

The gambling continued when the new man made no concessions to the orthodox in his choice of assistant manager. Most people in his position, having been out of the game and out of the country for so long, would have looked immediately for someone who had been employed at the higher levels of English football throughout his own eight-year 'sabbatical' and whose knowledge of it was bang up to date. Instead, Keegan put his faith in an old mate who had lost touch with the game to almost the same extent as he himself had. Terry McDermott's record as an attacking midfielder with Newcastle (twice), Liverpool and England was beyond question, but he had slipped into anonymity after following Keegan into retirement in 1984.

McDermott's exact circumstances before rejoining Newcastle for a second time remain a little vague, and I cannot throw much light on them because he declined to be interviewed for this book out of loyalty to Keegan. Some have him settling into a gentle retirement of playing golf, snooker and tennis, while others say he was earning a living supplying VIP catering at racecourses.

THE SECOND COMING

Perhaps he was doing a bit of both. What is not in doubt is that Terry 'Mac', as he is known to all and sundry, jumped at the chance of helping to save Newcastle from relegation when Keegan rang to offer him the assistant's job. 'I would have come in and helped make the tea if necessary,' McDermott was quoted as saying.

The loyalty implicit in McDermott's reluctance to talk to me about his part in the great adventure at Newcastle was exactly what Keegan was looking for in an assistant. 'The biggest thing Kevin wanted was loyalty and trust, and he knew he'd get that from McDermott,' says John Gibson. 'Terry always said that the day Keegan left he would too; but, amazingly, he didn't. He stayed on as assistant to Kenny Dalglish, another old mate from his Liverpool playing days. As it happens, I think Kevin persuaded him not to leave, because he hasn't made the sort of money Keegan has out of football. So losing his job, just because Kevin was chucking it in, was going to be difficult for him.'

Even so, loyalty and trust would have seemed in many eyes to be poor substitutes for the lack of technical expertise that McDermott brought to the table. For, like Keegan himself, the madcap Scouser had no coaching qualifications or experience to speak of. Since neither were technically equipped to take a training session and both had been out of the game for so long, most of the footballing fraternity sat back and waited for them to fall flat on their faces. 'Terry has told me many times since,' reveals John Gibson, 'that people in football thought Newcastle United had gone off their brains and appointed two jokes in himself and Kevin. They thought one was a retired golfer and the other a sandwich maker from Merseyside.

'He said he knew some were sniggering behind their backs, but he felt the board had very much had the last laugh with what the two of them achieved at St James' Park. They proved, against all the obvious odds, that they could actually do the job. Even though some might see them as the Odd Couple, there's no question, whatever anybody says, that they did prove they could be a highly successful management team. They were very,

very close to each other the whole time. So close, they were like twins. Terry was hugely loyal, and Kevin always looked for loyalty in the people around him. If they gave him loyalty, he was very loyal to them: that was one of his major traits. But never abuse that loyalty, because if you do, you are finished.'

Keegan and McDermott *were* something of an odd couple, in that their friendship was almost an attraction of opposites. Horse-racing is their main common interest outside football, but while Keegan likes a gamble as much as the next man, he was drawn to the sport more by the skills of breeding and training than by the betting urge that exerted its pull heavily on McDermott. They were certainly poles apart when it came to enjoying themselves socially. McDermott is – or was – a man who likes his pint, while Keegan, if he drinks at all, would probably prefer a white wine. Temperamentally, too, they are dissimilar. McDermott's harum-scarum, devil-may-care nature is pointed up by the intensity and careful planning Keegan has brought to his own life and career.

What united them more than anything was a shared sense of humour. There were two outstanding examples of it while they were players with Newcastle. In one case, when there was speculation about the Arabs wanting to buy Keegan, Terry Mac dressed up very convincingly as a sheik and travelled with his mate to St James' in a limousine. Then, when Arthur Cox's militaristic approach to training began to get the two of them down, Keegan and McDermott donned army uniforms and staged a mock raid on the training ground. It is not unreasonable to speculate, therefore, that McDermott had the knack of releasing the lighter, fun-loving side of Keegan's nature.

Both Derek Fazackerley and Mark Lawrenson believe that ability was of crucial importance in the relationship. Fazackerley, first-team coach for four years under Keegan, says, 'Terry was good for Kevin. One of Kevin's problems was that his highs were so high and his lows so low. And when Kevin was low, Terry could lift him by his personality. So, from that point of view, I thought they were a good mix.'

THE SECOND COMING

'Kevin has a real good sense of fun,' says Lawrenson, another former Liverpool player who eventually became part of the backroom staff at Newcastle, 'and Terry Mac was always conscious of that as a player. Terry made Kevin laugh and was a really good foil for him when they became partners in management.' He adds, 'Kevin is a man of extreme moods and, in the short time I was there, I could see that Terry Mac would be at him on his low days, trying to wind him up and get him going. They'd play things like head tennis together and wallyball, a game they'd kind of invented.

'Wallyball was a cross between squash and football. The rules were virtually the same as squash, except you played the ball – a football or a soft ball of some sort – with your head, your feet and any part of your body but your hands. It became a ritual on a Friday morning, or the day before a game. Kevin was probably the best at it. He had the best touch and was helped by the fact that he has such a low centre of gravity. The two of them used to take on all-comers and have all sorts of bets. It was good for morale. The coaching staff played wallyball more than anyone and they'd take on the players and wind them up. Kevin and Terry, as a pair, were also probably unbeatable at head-tennis; they would cheat fairly.

'Even if you had taken what they had done in football out of their relationship, I think they still would have been good mates. You probably have four or five really close friends you stay with throughout your life and I think Terry and Kevin come into that category with each other.'

It would be easy here to see McDermott as some sort of court jester, whose job amounted to not much more than coaxing King Kevin out of his black moods, but although the analogy is not a million miles wide of the mark, it does Terry Mac less than justice. As John Gibson points out, McDermott's usefulness to Keegan and Newcastle extended far beyond the delicate and crucial matter of keeping the boss's spirits up in times of stress.

'Certainly,' admits Gibson, 'Kevin christened Terry the "gofer" at first and didn't give him a title – assistant manager or whatever.

43

THE MAGNIFICENT OBSESSION

But he brought him in because he knew he was brilliant in the dressing-room. He saw him as a lifter of spirits. If Kevin blasted a player who deserved it, Terry would go and give him a cuddle and tell him the boss had a good point but he still rates you and thinks you are wonderful and can do this or do that. There are people who thought, at the start, Newcastle were just bringing in a clown to make people laugh and little else. But that was cruel and unfair. Although, like Kevin, Terry Mac couldn't be classed as a great coach, his reputation as a player went before him and earned him instant respect from even the superstars who eventually joined the club. He also had a huge network of contacts in the game and was very much the middleman for Kevin in transfer deals.'

Nor should it be forgotten that McDermott's was the voice that first persuaded Keegan to think again when Newcastle's impulsive new manager almost turned his back on St James' Park after only thirty-eight days in the job. With Keegan disillusioned by the board's failure, as he saw it, to live up to their promises about funding for new players ('It wasn't like it said in the brochure,' he said famously and witheringly about the situation), the pair of them checked out of the Gosforth Park Hotel, where they were staying, and hightailed it out of town. It was the Friday night before a game against Swindon on 14 March 1992, and it seems it was McDermott who persuaded Keegan to turn the car round and return to Newcastle to fulfil their responsibilities to the team the following day.

That was far from the end of the matter, however. Having seen Swindon beaten 3–1 and saying nothing to the players about their misgivings, Keegan left immediately afterwards for his home in Hampshire and McDermott returned to Merseyside. Heated negotiations were conducted on the Sunday by telephone with Sir John Hall at his home on the Wynyard Hall estate. Since Newcastle were £6.5 million in debt and Sir John was still fighting for outright control of the club, the chairman was in a difficult position. Ultimately, the crisis was averted when Sir John and his wife agreed to lodge a personal cheque of their own at the club and give their stubborn new manager the purchasing power he demanded. It was a crucial moment in Keegan's relationship with Newcastle. As Alan Oliver has observed: '... there is no doubt in my mind that on that Monday Keegan returned to Tyneside, the ground rules had been laid. Kevin Keegan was now bigger than the club.'

That may have been overstating the case a little, because it was not quite the straightforward battle of wills between Keegan and Hall that it might have appeared to be. The delay in making money available to Keegan was caused not by any stinginess or double-dealing on Sir John's part, but by the difficulties the chairman was encountering in trying to complete his takeover of the club. 'Kevin said I hadn't kept my promises and he went away and I was very surprised,' says Hall. 'But you have to remember we still didn't have complete control and the bank had a floating charge on all the assets of the club. Yes, I'd agreed to put some money in, but I wouldn't put it in until such time as we could guarantee it could be used to buy players. If I had put the money in straight away, it would have gone to pay off the debts.

'Kevin thought it was taking too long, as it probably was, and felt he had to protect himself. So he walked out. I rang him up and said, "Kevin, you know, it's only you who can sort it out." He came back and we sorted it out, but it wasn't straightforward at all. We had to put the legal mechanics into place, get the guarantees that the money could be used for players, like we'd planned, or else it was just feeding the hole of debt and not giving Kevin what he wanted.'

At the very least, Keegan had done what all good managers must and demonstrated beyond doubt that he would do the job only on his conditions. In purely practical terms, it was a show of strength and determination that was absolutely necessary if Keegan was to overcome the twin problems of a 'split' board and a team urgently in need of reconstruction. With Newcastle floundering near the bottom of the old Second Division and only three months of the 1991–92 season remaining, he knew only immediate action would give him a chance of pulling off a successful rescue operation. There was simply no time to waste if he was to drag a team and a club he had described as a 'shambles' back from the precipice leading to the former Third Division, ignominy and, almost certainly, financial disaster.

In Ossie Ardiles' last match as manager, as we know, Newcastle had lost 5–2 at Oxford – another attractive, attacking performance undermined by the habitual defensive frailty that lost the little Argentine his job. So, when Keegan began with a 3–0 home win against Bristol City, the chairman got a bit carried away. Conscious of the £10 million rescue scheme that had been in the offing, Sir John was quoted as saying: 'This has put the smile back on the faces of our backers. When we lost to Oxford United, the money for the rescue plan disappeared. We ran some projections through the computer and this victory [the attendance of 29,263 was nearly 14,000 up on the previous home game against Charlton] confirmed that the club could not exist if we were relegated. Now I'm confident we can survive.'

The chairman could be forgiven his early optimism. Everyone at Newcastle was conscious that some sort of sea-change had taken place with the appointment of Keegan as manager. No one was better placed to sense this than Derek Fazackerley, who had worked as a coach under two previous managers, Jim Smith and Ossie Ardiles. 'Jim had done a decent job there without the financial resources that were eventually to be made available to Kevin,' says Fazackerley. 'So his hands were tied behind his back a little bit in the respect that there was also some disharmony between the board and Sir John Hall, who was trying to gain control of the club at that particular time.

'It took quite a while to resolve itself, and there was quite a degree of uncertainty about the club's future. Obviously, that applied to the playing staff, coaching staff and everything. Then Kevin came in and it was a bit unique because of his own relationship with the supporters and the respect they had for him as a player. That sort of ignited the whole thing. The average gate went up from something like 21–22,000 to full houses, which at that time was about 27–28,000. It was just on the strength of Kevin, really. It had nothing to do with

THE SECOND COMING

what was going on on the football field: they came to watch Kevin be the manager. I think that fired everybody up, really, plus Kevin's enthusiasm for wanting to be successful.'

It was hardly plain sailing, however. Two of the next four games were lost and only one of them, away to fellow-strugglers Port Vale, was won. So, on 7 March, only eight weeks from the end of the season, Newcastle were still only one place above the three-team relegation zone. Gradually, however, the experience of two of Keegan's first signings began to exert an influence. While Kevin Sheedy, a free transfer, brought to the midfield the intuition and educated left foot that had served Everton so well for so many years, Brian 'Killer' Kilcline gave the defence the backbone it had lacked so disastrously under Ardiles.

Kilcline proved to be a particularly sound investment with the money Sir John and Lady Hall had made available to stop Keegan walking out for good. Although the hulking, hirsute centre back had appeared to be past his best when Coventry sold him to Oldham earlier that season, Newcastle's new management team felt he still had sufficient defensive solidity left to justify a £250,000 fee. Though Kilcline could hardly be said to have made the defence impregnable, he patched up enough of the holes for Keegan to credit him with doing more than any other player to save Newcastle from relegation.

Attacking midfielder Gavin Peacock and striker David Kelly were entitled to feel a little miffed at missing out on that accolade. Between them, Peacock and Kelly scored twenty-seven of the sixty-six League goals that preserved Newcastle's Second Division status, most of them coming in those vital last three months of the season. It was Peacock and Kelly who scored the two goals at Cambridge on 10 March that launched a run of three wins in four matches, for instance; and the same two players came good again in the final two, decisive games after Newcastle had suffered five consecutive defeats and looked to be slipping back towards the abyss.

That potentially disastrous run began with a 6–2 hammering by Wolverhampton Wanderers at Molineux on 31 March and ended with another heavy away defeat, 4–1 at Derby, on 20

THE MAGNIFICENT OBSESSION

April. Worse still, Newcastle had three players – Kevin Scott, Kevin Brock and Liam O'Brien – sent off and Terry McDermott cautioned, while Keegan himself even fell out with his great friend Arthur Cox, the former Newcastle manager who had taken over at Derby, in the sort of touchline fracas that was to be repeated more than once during his high-octane managerial career. Perhaps nothing indicated the pressure of the situation, the impending sense of doom, more clearly than the misbehaviour of Newcastle players and officials alike on that bad day at the Baseball Ground.

However, relief was just another fixture away. Kelly, the Republic of Ireland international who has given several clubs good service without really settling anywhere, claimed the solitary late goal that beat Portsmouth at St James' in the penultimate League game of the season. Then a scrambled effort by Peacock, who was later to enliven the Chelsea team after returning to his native south, put Newcastle ahead for practically the whole of the last match, away to Leicester on 2 May. It was not quite enough, since Steve Walsh, typically the heroic inspiration of a Leicester team trying to win promotion, equalized in the last minute. However, there was still one final dramatic twist to the story, poor Walsh turning the ball into his own net during the time added on for stoppages.

Even then, Newcastle were not quite sure whether they had survived. Walsh's own goal prompted a pitch invasion by the Leicester fans, and the players were led off the field by referee David Elleray. Was the match over or not? When Elleray finally confirmed that it was, a relieved Keegan discovered he had done the job he had been asked to do back in February. Newcastle had avoided, by four points, the ignominy of relegation to the old Third Division for the first time. They eventually finished in twentieth place, above Oxford United and the three relegated clubs, Plymouth Argyle, Brighton & Hove Albion and Port Vale. But that represented only qualified success, only a starting point, to someone with the high standards and burning ambition of Kevin Keegan.

4

ASCENSION

For all the Geordie euphoria over escaping relegation in the 1991–92 season, there was no certainty that Keegan would be back at St James' Park as manager for the start of the following season. He and McDermott had agreed to run the Newcastle team only until the end of the previous season and some serious negotiating was required before the two of them were prepared to commit themselves more fully to the task. Above all, they wanted guarantees that money for strengthening the side – the great bone of contention between manager and board during the fight to stay in the old Second Division – would be available in much greater quantities than before.

Sure enough, such guarantees were readily forthcoming from Douglas Hall when he and his trusty sidekicks, Freddie Shepherd and Freddie Fletcher, flew to Marbella in late May to talk to Keegan and his wife at their luxurious Spanish bolt-hole and persuade him to continue as manager. Emboldened, no doubt, by the success they had had in finally winning complete control of the club, the Halls promised Keegan a £2 million transfer fund and offered him a three-year contract at £120,000 a year, an eminently respectable salary for a Second Division manager in 1992. What is more, there was a three-year contract for Terry McDermott, whom Keegan had been paying out of his own pocket up to then.

The generosity of the terms reflected not only Newcastle's anxiety to keep Keegan, but also their realization that the newly formed, breakaway Premier League was the only place to be for a club with a huge fan base and soaring ambitions such as theirs. As hardly needs repeating, the Premier League is basically the former First Division of the Football League in a new guise. The essential difference is that, by leaving what was felt to be the suffocating embrace of a 92-club Football League, the elite won control of their own affairs. That gave them the freedom to negotiate the customized television, advertising and sponsorship contracts which have made the Premier League one of the richest domestic leagues in the world.

The Premier League championship, the Premiership, was about to be launched in August 1992 and the new, united, imaginative and canny Newcastle board were fully aware of its financial potential. Not only that, but everyone at St James' believed passionately that the club's rightful place was in the highest echelon of English football. No one believed it more than Keegan, for whom only the best would ever do. So, there cannot be any doubt at all that he began the new season with promotion from the First Division, as the former Second Division was now called following the formation of the Premier League, as his number one priority.

For the time being, however, Keegan contented himself with pledging his future to the club. Pleased with the outcome of the negotiations with Douglas Hall and the two Freddies, Keegan issued a statement that must have delighted the fans back in Newcastle with both its good news and its overtones of a new and much-needed stability. 'I wanted to come back if everything was right,' said the statement. 'Things had been happening at St James' Park [the boardroom upheavals] which had nothing to do with me, but now all the uncertainty has been lifted. I'm cutting short my stay in Spain to fly to Newcastle on Tuesday and begin work. My heart has always been with Newcastle and what has happened now is good for the club, good for the fans and good for Kevin Keegan, All the differences have been removed and I'm happy. I'll be moving my family to the north, lock, stock and barrel.'

Indeed, Keegan was delighted to accept Sir John's invitation to make yet another new family home in a plush house, near the chairman's own, on the accommodating Wynyard Hall estate. He was also greatly encouraged by the willingness of Newcastle's three musketeers – Douglas Hall and the two Freddies – to delay their trip back to Newcastle from Marbella and fly to Aix-en-Provence instead. The purpose of the unscheduled trip was to explore the possibility of arranging the transfer of Chris Waddle back to Newcastle from Marseilles, the French club with whom the former sausage factory worker had appeared in the European Cup final not long before. Although the idea did not reach fruition – despite Waddle's interest in returning home – the very fact that the new Newcastle board were prepared to give it serious consideration was the clearest possible indication to Keegan of how much things had changed at the club since the previous, stressful season.

Suddenly, after the struggle to avoid relegation to the old Third Division and possible oblivion, everything seemed set fair for a campaign to win promotion to the new Shangri-La of English football, the Premier League. Even so, such naked ambition was hardly conventional. As Derek Fazackerley puts it, 'Once we'd avoided relegation, Kevin's first words the next season were, "We want to be promoted." You go into some football clubs and, start of the season, it's a case of, "If we do this and get ourselves thirty-odd points, then we'll go on from there." But consolidation wasn't the way with Kevin. He just wanted to get promoted and do it in style. He also had this ability to drive people to the same goals.'

Keegan certainly wasted no time in putting to good use the transfer funds that were made available to him, as promised by the board. In the three months between 16 June and 22 September 1992, he spent a total of £1.85 million on four players who were to be the heart and soul of the first Newcastle side that could truly be called his. They were Paul Bracewell (£250,000 from Sunderland), John Beresford (£650,000 from Portsmouth), Barry Venison (£250,000 from Liverpool) and Robert Lee (£700,000 from Charlton).

In contrast with Keegan's first, desperate ventures into the transfer market a year earlier, all were first-class signings. The recruitment of Bracewell gave the Newcastle fans added pleasure because he had been lured away from North East rivals Sunderland, whom he had just captained in the FA Cup final. More importantly, the industrious Midlander, then a month short of his thirtieth birthday, brought to Newcastle's midfield the steadiness and experience of a man who had played with distinction alongside Peter Reid for both Everton and England. It did not do Bracewell any harm, either, when he scored the opening goal of the new season, at home against Southend. Venison, though only twenty-seven at the time, came into much the same category as Bracewell. Having made more than a hundred appearances for both Sunderland and Liverpool, the enthusiastic, versatile defender offered more of the class and experience Newcastle's new manager clearly felt his side needed. Not only that, but the Consett-born Venison was returning to his roots with something to prove.

Beresford, twenty-five, and Lee, twenty-six, though only slightly younger than Venison, were more speculative buys. Beresford, small, quick and a good crosser of the ball, had finally caught the eye at Portsmouth after failing to make the grade as an apprentice at Manchester City and then moving on more successfully to Barnsley. Keegan looked to be taking a real chance on the attacking left back, since Liverpool had just called off Beresford's projected transfer to Anfield because of a suspected ankle injury. But the former Liverpool player, with typical self-belief and independence of mind, chose to ignore the scare stories about Beresford's medical history and went ahead and signed the defender.

While Beresford jumped at the chance of joining Newcastle after the disappointment he had suffered at Liverpool, Lee had to be cajoled into leaving the south of England. Born in West Ham, the sturdy, goal-scoring midfielder had spent the whole of his nine-year career with Charlton as they shuttled between the former Second and First divisions. Lee's attachment to London was so strong that not even Lennie Lawrence, the former Charlton manager, had been able to persuade him to go north after he had taken over at Middlesbrough in July 1991. Yet, somehow, Keegan managed to convince Lee that a move to Newcastle, more than thirty miles further north, was in his best interests. It is said he did it by stressing the speed and directness of the train service between Newcastle and King's Cross, but the recruitment of Lee has to be attributed, for the most part, to Keegan's sheer persuasiveness and characteristic determination to get what he wanted. And there was no way he was going to lose out on a player he later called, with typical understatement, 'the best in any position in England'.

By the time Lee arrived at St James' Park on 22 September 1992, Newcastle were already top of the table, a position they were to hold almost permanently for the rest of the season. They had fairly exploded out of the blocks with seven successive wins, scoring nineteen goals and conceding only five. Gavin Peacock and David Kelly were again prominent among the goalscorers, while Lee Clark, then only nineteen, and Liam O'Brien also weighed in from midfield. Nor did that dazzling burst of form end there. Another four wins enabled them to equal the club record, the achievement made all the sweeter by the fact that the eleventh consecutive opening victory came at Roker Park, home of arch-rivals Sunderland. 'We haven't changed anything massive in the way we play,' Keegan explained at the time. 'There is no way you can go so quickly from the bottom to the top. We have pushed Gavin Peacock forward, and have tried to play more in the opponents' half. But you can't make a system and say "play that way". You've got to suit the players in your team.'

Sir John Hall makes an interesting point here about the speed with which Keegan got to grips with the job of managing a big club in English football. 'We played in such an exciting way,' he says, 'that it was difficult to believe this man could actually generate that from being out of the game for a long time. He'd been out of the game, but he must have been always in the game in the sense that he probably studied it, read a lot and kept himself up-to-date with the pattern. He can't have really divorced himself from the game, because he knew players and he knew the style of play he wanted.'

Very few seasons are without setbacks, however, and Keegan's rampaging side were suddenly brought up short at the end of October by unexpected, back-to-back defeats against Grimsby at home and Leicester away. In between, Newcastle were also knocked out of the Coca-Cola Cup at Chelsea. It was a test of the players' character and Keegan's motivational powers and they passed it with flying colours. A hard-earned 3–2 win at Birmingham and a goalless draw at home with Swindon were followed by another four victories on the trot. The fourth of those wins, by 2–0 at Notts County, put Newcastle twelve points clear at the top of the new First Division at the beginning of December 1992, an advantage they still enjoyed over Tranmere Rovers as the New Year arrived.

Indeed, things were going so swimmingly that Keegan felt confident enough to tempt fate. Managing Newcastle United was an easy job, he said, because the players were a dream to handle – and the fact that they were playing to sell-out crowds at St James' Park would be a big benefit the following season, when the club were in the Premier League.

Keegan was such a masterly motivator that it would be unwise to dismiss those kind of statements as mere braggadocio. There is every reason to believe the manager's boasting was his calculated way of building up the players' confidence for the second half of a rigorous season. The danger, of course, is that saying such things can encourage complacency; and, in January 1993, with a goalless FA Cup tie at home against Second Division Port Vale, Keegan had to remind his players that they needed to do more than just go through the motions to succeed. Their response to his pointed remarks was a four-goal burst of scoring that brought Newcastle their biggest third-round win for nineteen years.

There were also signs of a certain faltering in the League. Between 20 January and 24 February, Newcastle did not win a single game. They drew five and lost one of their six fixtures

ASCENSION

and managed to score only two goals. Their lead at the top of the table, a massive fifteen points when they drew 1–1 at Southend on 20 January, was down to just four by the time they ground out a goalless draw at Upton Park on 21 February with West Ham, the club who were to finish second, eight points behind. Not long before the trip to London, too, Newcastle were knocked out of the FA Cup by Blackburn Rovers in a fifth-round tie at Ewood Park. During this relatively fallow period, Keegan celebrated his first anniversary as manager of the club. 'If they taught it [football management] at university,' he joked, 'they would set up a simulated course like I have had and people would say it's too far-fetched. But it's actually happened and I still believe it's only the start.'

His belief was renewed by the successive wins, away to Tranmere (3–0), one of Newcastle's promotion rivals, and at home to Brentford (5–1) at the end of February and beginning of March, which were the prelude to a final push for the title. Of the last thirteen fixtures, eight were won and only three lost. The most impressive aspect of the run-in was the five victories they reeled off to bring it to a close. During the sprint for the line, Barnsley were hammered 6–0 at St James' and the double was completed over Sunderland with a rain-sodden home victory that enabled Newcastle to reclaim the League leadership from Portsmouth, who had held it for a day after beating Wolves.

Promotion was actually secured at Grimsby on 4 May with two games still to play. Goals by Andy Cole (of whom more later) and Kelly gave Newcastle revenge for Grimsby's victory at St James', the only defeat suffered at home by the Magpies all season. More importantly, the win brought the two points that were needed to ensure a place in the Premier League the following season. No wonder, then, the excited Newcastle fans spilled on to the pitch when Cole opened the scoring, causing a six-minute hold-up, or that an exuberant, jubilant Kelly tipped the physio's bucket of cold water over Keegan after scoring the second, clinching goal in injury time.

So, after an uninspired 2–1 win over Oxford at St James' two days later, the scene was set for a proper celebration in the last match, at home to Leicester, the club against whom Newcastle had struggled to stay up at Filbert Street in the final game of the previous season. Now, by contrast, it was carnival time. Assured of the First Division championship and promotion, Keegan's team put on a real show. Six up at half-time, they eventually won 7–1 against one of the clubs who had made the play-offs. A packed St James' was delirious with joy, and some will always view the match as the defining moment of Keegan's stewardship.

'I doubt if I've ever, in the whole of my life – not just covering Newcastle, but World Cups, England, everything – seen such an amazing forty-five minutes as that first half against Leicester,' says John Gibson. 'It was amazing not only because of what happened on the field, but also because of the fans' reaction to it. That forty-five minutes will certainly stand as a monument in my mind to what Kevin Keegan represented to this area.'

Three of Newcastle's seven goals that day were scored by Cole, the striker Keegan had signed from Bristol City for £1.75 million just before the March transfer deadline as a guarantee of promotion. Cole's potential had been spotted by Keegan and McDermott while Newcastle were beating City at home and away that season and they were not put off by the stories that Arsenal had let him go because of his bad attitude. Again, as in the case of John Beresford, Keegan ignored the rumours and backed his own judgement. His immediate reward was the twelve goals Cole scored in as many appearances during those critical last two months of the season. Many of his scoring chances were provided by Scott Sellars, the left-sided midfielder Keegan had bought from Leeds for £700,000 and another outstanding example of his eye for underrated talent. Sellars, also signed shortly before the transfer deadline, was not just a provider, either. The free-kick he whipped over Sunderland's wall in the monsoon match has guaranteed him immortality on Tyneside.

What is not so well known is that Sir John Hall bought Andy Cole for Newcastle with his own money at a time when the club

ASCENSION

didn't have any. He made the decision while in the bath and ruminating about how he could help clinch promotion. 'The bath's always a good place to think about things, I always find,' he says, 'and I'm thinking to myself that we've got to get promotion, get this finally built, it's more difficult every year, Liverpool's always bought at the top. So I got out of the bath and said to my wife, "Mae, we've got to buy Andy Cole and you're going to have to fund this one." She said, "What!". £1.75 million I think it cost us. The club had a couple of hundred thousand and I think we put in £1.5 million.

'Kevin didn't know anything about it at the time. But I knew Andy was the player he wanted most. So I said to Freddie Fletcher, "Buy Andy Cole." He rang Bristol City at 9.30 in the morning, but City had so many directors in those days, it took them a while to make a decision. I thought to myself that we were never going to get a decision out of this lot, but it just happened that they were having a board meeting at the time. They had been holding us to ransom previously: first they wanted £1.1 million, then it was £1.2, £1.4 and so on. So I told them the final offer was £1.75 and they had thirty minutes to make up their minds. They came back in fifteen and said yes. That was how cavalier and entrepreneurial we were in those days. That's what you had to be at that moment in time. You had to push Newcastle United through really hard if you wanted to be with the giants of soccer.'

Newcastle scored ninety-two League goals in all that season – far more than anyone else in the four divisions of English football. This was the time when they first began to acquire a reputation for the attacking football that excited football lovers beyond Tyneside. Rotherham, for instance, got their first capacity gate for twenty-two years when they drew Newcastle at home in the fourth round of the FA Cup. But those who were at the heart of things insist there was nothing calculated, nothing deliberate, about it in the sense that Keegan did not issue orders as to how the team should play. It was more a question of the style evolving naturally from the players who were available. 'I don't think you could say it was Kevin's idea to play in that way,' says Derek Fazackerley. 'Having avoided relegation, money was made available to him in the summer and he bought certain players. So it was something that developed over a period of time. I don't think anybody sort of sat down and consciously said, "Right, we want to play this way."

'Obviously, we had players who were very comfortable on the ball and could handle themselves in the kick and rush atmosphere – if that's what you want to call it – of First Division football. That season [1992–93] they were a street ahead of anybody else in the division. As much as anything, their style of play excited the fans; and the fans, in their own way, fuelled the team. It was as though they sparked off each other. It was something that generated itself. It's very difficult to say what sparked it off, or why it happened. It was just a unique period and it was all down to Kevin going back as the manager. I don't think anybody could have envisaged somebody being out of football for eight years, or whatever it was, going back to a football club and taking it from the lower reaches of the old Second Division, as it was then, into the Premier League.'

At this stage, the defence was not a problem. Newcastle conceded only thirty-eight goals in forty-six games – fewer than any of their rivals at the top of the table – on their way to winning the First Division title. It represented a marked improvement on the previous season when, mostly under the excessively adventurous management of Ossie Ardiles, a staggering total of eighty-four goals had been let in. One of the reasons for the greater solidity at the back, almost certainly, was the promotion to first-team coach of Fazackerley by Keegan. A former salt-of-the-earth centre half whose 596 League appearances between 1970 and 1986 still constitute a club record in his native Blackburn, Fazackerley was exactly the sort of practical, yet flexible, figure Keegan needed to balance his own attacking instincts.

'If I sit and watch a game of football,' says Fazackerley, 'I like to get excited by good attacking play. But it's got to be measured and calculated. Probably, from that point of view,

ASCENSION

I'd be different from Kevin or Terry. I'd be a little bit more cautious about things; but that's the way you are when you are an ex-defender. I'd like to think I had some input into the way the team played, and the organization of it. You can't just pick eleven players and send them out to play: it doesn't happen like that in football. You need some sort of organization.

'The season before, they had conceded all those goals under Ossie Ardiles, but the year we were promoted, we had as good a defensive record as anybody in the country. Even so, we weren't a side that was noted for its defensive strength. Because of all the goals we scored [ninety-two in the League] and the introduction of Andy Cole and Scott Sellars, we were known as a team that played attractive football. The defence perhaps didn't get the credit it deserved, because there were times when they had to dig in a little bit and they showed they had the character to do it. Because of all the attacking play, that very often got overlooked.'

Fazackerley's value to the great enterprise that took shape under Keegan was widely recognized, however. The large number of interviews with him that appeared in the broadsheet newspapers was one measure of his importance in the eyes of the thinking outside world and there was never any danger he would be under-valued on Tyneside. John Gibson offers the close-up view when he says, 'Faz was the great survivor, and there was a strong body of opinion that while he was at Newcastle the defence was better.

'Kevin always said that when he was a player at Liverpool and Bill Shankly talked in the dressing-room about the defence and the midfield, he didn't listen. He tied his boots, because defence and midfield didn't concern him. Only when it came to the forwards would he listen. And he brought that attitude – let's win 4–3 – to St James' Park. But Faz, as a former defender, was very much aware of defensive responsibilities; and while he had to work within the Keegan framework, which was all-out attack, he would have safeguards. There was certainly a feeling that when Faz went in 1995, perhaps some of the defensive soundness went with him. Which I think was eventually recognized by Keegan when he brought in Mark Lawrenson.'

Newcastle's greater solidity in defence during the 1992–93 season was not simply a question of better organization. It must not be forgotten that Keegan, a manager with a supposed blind spot when it came to defence, had bought Venison and Beresford specifically to slot into the full-back positions. They played either side of the reliable, long-serving Kevin Scott and Steve Howey, one of the club's many emerging young talents. It was Howey who supplanted Brian Kilcline, the defensive giant of Newcastle's successful fight to avoid relegation to the old Third Division. But Kilcline, on whom they recouped £100,000 of the modest, original fee of £250,000 when they sold him to Swindon early in 1994, had helped to lay the foundations Keegan needed to pursue his dream of winning things in style.

'As Newcastle United got bigger and bigger,' explains John Gibson, 'they bought bigger and bigger, and Kevin's dream of being able to play this fantasy football became stronger and stronger. To start with, he had to build with what he had and would buy players for small money, like Brian Kilcline. But the whole thing couldn't have happened without Kilcline. Having got the platform provided by "Killer" and the defence organized by Derek Fazackerley, Kevin could go on and indulge his fantasy.'

No one could deny, however, the magnitude of Keegan's achievement. To have taken Newcastle into the Premier League only a season after saving them from relegation to the former Third Division was a truly monumental effort. It could be argued that he was given the money to do it, but any money has to be spent wisely in order to have an effect on the field. Not only that, but Keegan had done it with little or no first hand experience of management.

Those closest to him were not surprised by the speed of their friend's success. Arthur Cox, the manager who had brought him to St James' Park as a player and became a lifelong buddy, said,

ASCENSION

'Right at the start, when Keegan was made Newcastle manager, I predicted he would succeed. It's in his nature. Outwardly, he gives the impression of looking relaxed and confident. But inside Kevin is a cold, hard professional. Mark my words, he's a bad, bad loser. And I should know, because Kevin is the only person in football I've ever had a close relationship with.'

Not surprisingly, Keegan's dramatic revival of Newcastle renewed the speculation about his becoming manager of England. Only a month after the promotion celebrations and the trouncing of Leicester at St James' Park on 9 May 1993, the incumbent national team manager, Graham Taylor, saw his side easily beaten 2–0 by Norway in Oslo. It proved to be a crucially damaging result in England's qualifying campaign for the 1994 World Cup and the effect was not improved by losing embarrassingly to the USA by the same score in Boston a week later. Taylor was also an England manager still recovering from the obloquy of having substituted the England captain and icon, Gary Lineker, towards the end of a particularly unsuccessful stab at the 1992 European Championship finals.

'I'm sure he's ready-made to take over from Graham Taylor without gaining Premier League experience,' insisted Cox. 'Kevin's got that Pied Piper touch. People respond to his enthusiasm and knowledge as a former world-class player.' Mick Channon, Keegan's old horse-racing mate from the playing days with Southampton, Newcastle and England, was of the same opinion. 'Kevin takes a distant view of horse-racing these days in the same way I take a distant view of the soccer scene,' said Channon, by then a horse trainer. 'But I've seen and heard enough to know his right to the international job is a racing certainty, a foregone conclusion.'

5

ONWARDS AND UPWARDS

Mick Channon could not have been much wider of the mark if he had tried. Far from seeking the managership of England, or being offered it, Keegan quickly set about the task of equipping Newcastle for the rigorous challenge of playing against the best club sides in England. First, he cleared the decks by selling five players for a total of £2.45 million. Most prominent among them were David Kelly and Gavin Peacock, the strikers whose combined haul of thirty-six League goals had made such a telling contribution to the promotion campaign. It cannot have been an easy decision to sell those two popular players, if only because it risked the wrath of the fans. But one thing Keegan was never afraid to do was grasp the nettle.

Exactly why the Newcastle manager decided to sell Kelly to Wolves for £750,000 only he can tell. After all, the itinerant Irishman had finished the previous season, like Andy Cole, by scoring a hat-trick in the 7–1 goal-fest against Leicester. No doubt the signing of Cole and the prospective signing of Peter Beardsley had something to do with it. As for Peacock, there was a compassionate dimension to his £1.25 million transfer to Chelsea in that he wanted to return to London with his family. Keegan also sold Northern Ireland international goalkeeper Tommy Wright to Nottingham Forest for £450,000 the day after he had bought Mike Hooper from Liverpool for £550,000.

Hooper was one of five purchases – most of them unexceptional, it must be said – that Keegan made during the close season and in the early part of the 1993–94 season at a combined cost of £2.48 million. The second-choice goalkeeper (behind

THE MAGNIFICENT OBSESSION

Pavel Srnicek) was certainly not the manager's most popular acquisition: in fact, Keegan threatened to resign at one point because of the abuse the accident-prone Hooper was having to take from the fans. But there was one gold nugget in among all the dross. That was Beardsley.

By July 1993, the little Geordie genius had ended up playing for Everton, with his customary distinction, after Kenny Dalglish – rather strangely – had decided he could afford to let him leave Liverpool in 1991. No doubt Beardsley's age – he was thirty when he moved across Stanley Park to Everton for £1 million – had a bearing on Dalglish's decision. So Keegan had some convincing to do when he asked the Newcastle board to stump up £1.5 million for a player who was halfway towards his thirty-third birthday at the time the manager wanted to take him back home as his answer to the Premiership challenge.

While fully aware of Beardsley's ability, Sir John Hall was understandably reluctant to pay more than £1 million for a player who was well over thirty and might have no sell-on value. Keegan, however, was absolutely certain that Beardsley's skill and experience would be the key to Newcastle's survival and success in the Premiership. So he played a card from the bottom of the deck: he told the Newcastle board that hated rivals Sunderland had also made a bid for the Everton striker. This was completely untrue, but it did the trick. It hardly matters whether Sir John fell for the story or simply used it as a get-out: the money was made available for Beardsley's transfer back to his native Newcastle.

'Peter was magical at times,' says Chris McMenemy, who joined the coaching staff at more or less the same time that Beardsley was signed from Everton. 'He was rejuvenated as a player. He was also the one person who'd won something as a player, come back and said publicly that he was grateful to come back. There were young lads in the team like Andy Cole, Lee Clark, Steve Watson and Darren Peacock, some of whom had the difficult experience of justifying a large transfer fee, and Peter bonded them all together. He really was Kevin on

ONWARDS AND UPWARDS

the field. All the successful teams have had someone of whom the manager could say, "That's my eyes and ears", and Peter was Kevin's. He could set an example on the field because of the way he is as a person – professional and what you'd want your own son to be in a lot of ways.'

Not that Keegan's success in signing Beardsley initially benefited the team or the player much. Having done Ronnie Whelan a favour by taking a team to Anfield for the veteran Republic of Ireland international's testimonial just before the season started, the Newcastle manager watched in horror and anger as Beardsley's cheekbone was broken in a clash with the burly, aggressive Liverpool defender, Neil Ruddock. It meant that Beardsley, who contemplated suing Ruddock, would miss the first four of five weeks of the new season. So Keegan, ever the pragmatist, went out and paid Millwall £300,000 for Malcolm Allen, the Welsh international striker, as a stop-gap replacement for his injured star.

Allen must have been pinching himself silly when he ran out at St James' Park on 14 August 1993 as part of a Newcastle team playing its first game in the Premiership. The setting was perfect. The sun shone and the ground was packed. Not the old Victorian St James', but a semi-modernized version. By the start of the 1993–94 season, Newcastle had completed the new North Stand at the old Leazes End as part of their £27 million reconstruction of the stadium and it looked a treat. I know, because I covered the game.

It was quite a story for us hacks in that Newcastle then contrived to lose 1–0 to none other than a Tottenham team managed by Ossie Ardiles, the manager who had been sacked to make way for Keegan. Teddy Sheringham scored the goal that offered Ardiles some emotional recompense for his summary dismissal by the Newcastle board, and Liam O'Brien hit a post with a free-kick in the closing seconds after coming on as substitute for Allen. Clearly, on Newcastle's return to the big time, it was not meant to be their day.

The second game was lost, too. Keegan's men were beaten

2–1 at Coventry by a late goal from Mick Harford, a former Newcastle striker. So they could hardly be said to have gone to Old Trafford on the second Saturday of the season brimming with confidence for their first look at Manchester United, the reigning champions. When Ryan Giggs lashed in a free-kick shortly before the interval, it looked all over. But in the second half, the Cypriot Nicky Papavasilou, one of Keegan's cheaper and less celebrated summer signings, put Andy Cole through for the equalizer. And that draw was a definite turning-point.

Asked, at season's end, when he knew Newcastle were going to be a force in the Premiership, Keegan replied, 'On the second Saturday of the season at Old Trafford. We had lost our first two games and we were expected to lose to the champions. I simply told the players that I believed in them. All they had to do was believe in themselves. They then went out and took a point from Manchester United they richly deserved; and, after that, we had no problem with their confidence.'

It was a prime example of Keegan's gift for inspiring others, getting the best out of them. Chris McMenemy marvels at it. McMenemy, the Geordie son of Lawrie, joined Newcastle's back-room staff as chief scout, then director of youth football, in the summer of 1993 – just after they had won promotion to the Premier League – following six years as manager of Chesterfield. Two years later, Keegan appointed him to replace Derek Fazackerley as first-team coach when Fazackerley decided to return to Blackburn in the same capacity. It was a position McMenemy occupied until Kenny Dalglish recruited the former Celtic manager, Tommy Burns, as a coach in the summer of 1997. So few have had a closer look at Keegan's motivational techniques.

'When Kevin was a player,' says McMenemy, 'they were never taught how to manage people, how to motivate them. You'd always done it for yourself, or the manager had done it for you. Yet Kevin was probably the best motivator I've ever come across. It didn't matter whether it was with individuals or groups. Managing a group of people is a difficult thing to do if you've never been trained to do it, but it came naturally to Kevin. I wonder whether the time he had out of the game helped, because he didn't have to go straight from playing to management. Maybe that time out gave him a broader scope of knowledge.

'Some managers, you go into team meetings and they are very organized, telling the players what to do. Kevin was obviously organized, too, otherwise he wouldn't have got what he wanted, but you would come out of his team meetings really wanting to go out and give everything. It was the inspiration behind the way Newcastle played. Kevin would talk to you as a manager and you would realize he was desperate to be out there and playing in that game. And that was reflected in the players' performances, I think. They were all effervescent and eager to go forward. The players who'd never really achieved a great deal in the game would benefit most. All of a sudden, they were being regarded as attacking players with flair, when it was really just the personality of Kevin Keegan coming through. He was unbelievable at doing that.'

Under the circumstances, it was no surprise when Newcastle secured their first Premiership victory in the next match, a home game against Everton, with a goal by Allen. There were only three more wins in the next eight League games, though, as Keegan's team consistently struggled to come to terms with the greater demands of the higher level of competition. An example of just how raw the nerve ends had become by 24 October was an unedifying, but revealing, little scene on the touchline at The Dell, where Newcastle lost 2–1. When Keegan substituted Lee Clark, the young midfielder showed his annoyance by kicking physiotherapist Derek Wright's bag. Clark was stalking off down the touchline toward the dressing-rooms when a furious Keegan gave chase and dragged him back to the dug-out. It was a glimpse of the iron fist in the velvet glove, and one which Clark never really recovered from having been shown.

His immediate punishment was to be dropped for the next match, a third-round Coca-Cola Cup tie at Wimbledon on 27

THE MAGNIFICENT OBSESSION

October, which just happened to be his twenty-first birthday. But Keegan had a lot more on his mind before the kick-off than this spat with his young midfielder. For Andy Cole, scorer of fifteen League and cup goals already, had gone missing from Newcastle's headquarters at Selsdon Park in south London. When the increasingly prolific striker was not in the team that took the field at Selhurst Park that night, word went round that he was suffering from a hamstring injury. At the press conference following the game, however, Keegan volunteered the information that Cole had gone AWOL, and invited the football writers to go out into London and find him. This was yet another facet of his fascinating personality, the heart-on-the-sleeve approach to problems.

According to Alan Oliver in *Geordie Messiah*, Cole told the local newspaperman that he had had a row with Keegan. The manager, the striker claimed, had flown off the handle when he told him he was homesick, so Cole retorted by saying he did not want to play in the game against Wimbledon. The dispute proved so serious that it needed the intervention of the board's trouble-shooters, Douglas Hall and the two Freddies. Peace was not restored until the three directors met Cole and his agent, Paul Stretford, at Jesmond, a genteel Newcastle suburb. It ended, as Oliver observes, in smiles and handshakes all round; but Keegan was careful to publicly convey the message that he did not regret anything he had done. In other words, he was still the boss.

Confident his authority had not been undermined, Keegan restored Cole and Clark to the team for the next match. Ironically, it just happened to be a home League game against Wimbledon, the team who had knocked them out of the Coca-Cola Cup by winning 2–1 in the fraught circumstances at Selhurst Park three days earlier. Cole responded by scoring what was his now customary goal, but was overshadowed by a hat-trick from Peter Beardsley, who had returned the previous month more quickly than expected after his cheekbone injury. Wimbledon are such difficult opponents to overcome that few teams beat them 4–0, as Newcastle did on that occasion.

ONWARDS AND UPWARDS

Recognizing the significance of the result, Keegan predicted afterwards that his team were on course to become a real force in the game.

Anyone who might have interpreted that as sheer bravado was confounded by the three thumping victories which followed. Oldham were beaten 3–1 at Boundary Park before Liverpool and Sheffield United were trounced 3–0 and 4–0 respectively at St James' Park. The game at Oldham was shown live by Sky Television, and Newcastle's attacking play was so entrancing that it prompted anchorman Richard Keys to dub them 'the Entertainers'. Keegan loved that image because it was exactly the one he wanted his team to project. He can't have been too displeased, either, at hearing the ecstatic Newcastle fans chant, 'What's it like to be outclassed?' as a Cole hat-trick sank his manager's old club, Liverpool. It was a game which Liverpool goalkeeper Bruce Grobbelaar was alleged to have been bribed to help the opposition win, but you would have a hard job persuading Newcastle and their fans that the colourful, eccentric Zimbabwean international had anything to do with their team's emphatic victory.

That three-game winning streak took Newcastle up into a challenging position. By the start of December 1994, they had reached the dizzy heights of third place in the Premiership after beating Tottenham 2–1 at White Hart Lane. Then another draw with Manchester United, 1–1 at St James' Park, confirmed the right of Keegan's team to be contesting the major prize in English football with the best teams in the land. Results after that were a bit patchy until Newcastle suddenly hit their stride with a vengeance by beating Coventry 4–0 at home on 23 February. It was the first of six successive wins that established the Magpies firmly on the third-highest perch. In that blistering run, they scored twenty-one goals and conceded only three, the highlight being a 7–1 home win against Swindon, made unusual by the fact that Andy Cole did not score.

The next time Cole failed to find the net, against Chelsea at St James' Park five games later, was in Newcastle's first goalless draw for fifty-seven matches. Nothing could illustrate more vividly than that bare statistic the adventurous nature of the football Keegan's team played. But there was still a final flourish to come ... Winning all but one of their last five matches, Newcastle completed the double over Liverpool with a 2–0 victory at Anfield and hammered Aston Villa 5–1 at St James' Park. So, to general astonishment but fully on merit, they finished their first season in the Premiership in third place – seven points behind Blackburn Rovers and fifteen behind Manchester United. It was an extraordinary achievement, considering they had been within a whisker of dropping into the former Third Division only a couple of years earlier.

It was certainly an extraordinary period for Cole. The goal he scored in the 5–1 victory over Villa made him the first Newcastle player to amass forty goals in a season; and the one he got in the final game, a 2–0 win against his old club, Arsenal, gave him a staggering total of forty-one in the League and the two domestic cup competitions. Prompted cleverly by Beardsley and Clark from behind, and by Sellars from the left, Cole got to a point where he simply could not miss. His confidence was so high that every time he took aim at goal, it seemed, the ball flew into the net. Indeed, few could understand the reluctance of new England coach Terry Venables to put the Newcastle hot-shot straight into the national team.

Venables had been appointed in January 1994, to fill the vacancy left by the resignation of Graham Taylor in December 1993 because of England's failure to qualify for the finals of the 1994 World Cup. Venables' appointment must have come as a great relief to the Newcastle board and the club's fans, since it ended all the speculation about Keegan leaving to take the biggest job of all. But the Newcastle manager had virtually ruled himself out of contention already by signing a new, three-year contract with the club during the season and publicly declaring that he wasn't interested in taking over from Taylor when the unsuccessful England manager resigned.

And then, just a few days before the end of the 1993–94

ONWARDS AND UPWARDS

season, Keegan committed himself to Newcastle on almost an unprecedented scale. Signing a ten-year contract, he was, as Alan Oliver puts it, 'elevated from being a mere manager to United's Director of Football'. Keegan explained his momentous decision by saying the job felt right and he wanted to see it through. He was also anxious that the players should know he was totally committed to the club. But they must have guessed that from the moves he had made in the transfer market in the second half of the 1993–94 season. The recruitment of Norwich winger Ruel Fox (£2.25 million) and Queen's Park Rangers centre back Darren Peacock (£2.7 million) was evidence not only of the Newcastle board's continuing willingness to back their manager's judgement with hard cash, but also of Keegan's determination to make his team even stronger in defence as well as attack.

6

EUROPE AND ANDY

By finishing the 1993–94 Premiership season in third place – then their highest position in English football since the Second World War – Newcastle qualified for Europe. Not that they could be immediately sure of competing in the UEFA Cup the following season. This, remember, was at a time when the English representation in that particular club competition had been severely reduced as a result of the five-year ban imposed following the Heysel Stadium disaster in 1985. Because the English had been out in the cold for so long, they were still in the process of clawing back the qualification points required to put as many as five clubs in the field, as was the case in the last season before banishment, 1984–85. So Keegan and company had to sit and wait for a lucky break.

That break came a month after the end of the 1993–94 season, when the bloody civil war in Yugoslavia made it impossible for UEFA to include clubs from that now fragmented and brutalized country in the three European competitions. In June 1994, one of the vacancies went to Newcastle and they prepared for a return to the tournament they had won way back in 1968–69, when it was still known as the Inter-Cities Fairs Cup. So memories were stirred of Joe Harvey's splendid side, who had beaten the Hungarian Ujpest Dozsa 6–2 on aggregate in the two-legged final after scraping into the competition because of the one-club-per-city rule in effect at the time. That was the team which contained such outstanding players as Willie McFaul, Bobby Moncur, Frank Clark, Bryan 'Pop' Robson (the short, balding one) and Wyn Davies.

THE MAGNIFICENT OBSESSION

In fact, up to that point, the Fairs/UEFA Cup was the only major European tournament Newcastle had participated in. They had gone a long way in it the following season as defending champions before losing to Anderlecht of Belgium on the away goals rule, then were beaten on penalties by Pecsi Dozsa, another Hungarian side, in 1970–71. There was a further stab at it in 1977–78, but one which was ended fairly comprehensively in the second round by the French club Bastia. Keegan's side, of course, were expected to do better than that: Harvey's triumphant team had to be the benchmark, so far as the Toon Army was concerned.

And it all began so well. Newcastle staggered the whole of Europe by slaughtering Royal Antwerp, their Belgian opponents in the first round, 5–0 in the first, away leg. Allowances for the fact that Antwerp are not one of Europe's front-rank clubs aside, it was an extraordinarily emphatic victory by an English team making what was, in effect, its debut in European football. 'They went to Antwerp and tore them apart,' recalls Mark Lawrenson with relish, 'and you could see that coming. Watching them play, you could look at them and say they were going to give some good side a real thumping.'

Intriguingly, Newcastle won by relying on the all-out attacking methods which had served them so well in domestic football: the methods which most pundits, myself included, believed would not work in the more technically demanding context of European competition. Antwerp were blown away, almost literally, by the sheer gusto of their opponents' play as Newcastle went a goal up after only fifty seconds and scored twice more before the interval. Robert Lee came away from the game with an unusual hat-trick, in that all three of his goals were headers.

Understandably, Keegan was on top of the world that memorable night in Belgium. Alan Oliver, the *Evening Chronicle* man, reckons the Newcastle manager was more elated then than at any other time in his experience. In one of the impassioned outpourings that made him so football-writer-friendly, Keegan said what his team could achieve with performances like that was frightening. Terry McDermott, who had played in three of Liverpool's European Cup-winning teams, expressed the opinion that it was as good a one-off performance as he had ever seen in European football. An ecstatic Sir John Hall told anyone who cared to listen that this was the football of the future.

By 13 September 1994, everything was coming up roses for Keegan and McDermott. Before wiping the floor with Antwerp, Newcastle had won their first five games in the Premiership. St James' Park went mad as Coventry were beaten 4–0 and Southampton 5–1 in an opening run that yielded a goal difference of 19–5 as well as maximum points. Unsurprisingly, given form like that, Newcastle were now top of the Premiership for the first time since they had come up from the First Division the previous season.

It was not as though Keegan had strengthened the side dramatically during the summer, either. Philippe Albert, the versatile Belgian international, was the most expensive and most important of the signings Keegan made in his total spend of £3.88 million on him, Swiss international full back Marc Hottiger and two players who did not make the grade at St James' Park, Steve Guppy (from Wycombe) and Jason Drysdale (from Watford). Then, in late September, Keegan paid Derby £2.25 million for striker Paul Kitson in a transfer that was intended to strengthen the squad more than anything else.

Kitson was bought the day before Newcastle finished off Antwerp in the second leg of their tie at St James' Park. Keegan had been worried that his team's 5–0 lead from the first leg might make them complacent, but they completed the job in a thoroughly professional manner – a 5–2 victory producing an aggregate that was a club record in Europe and much better than the 6–2 by which Joe Harvey's side had won the same tournament twenty-five years earlier. Since three of United's second five goals against Antwerp came from Andy Cole, it meant that the increasingly deadly striker had become the first Newcastle player to score a hat-trick in three major competitions. Not even Malcolm Macdonald, old Supermac himself, had been able to manage that.

Newcastle were still unbeaten in the league and riding high at the top of the Premiership when Athletic Bilbao came to St James' Park on 18 October for the first leg of the second-round tie between the clubs. Again, Keegan's men got off to a flyer. An early goal from Ruel Fox and a penalty converted by Peter Beardsley sent them in at half-time leading 2–0. Then, early in the second half, a beautiful five-man move saw Cole increase Newcastle's lead to apparently unassailable proportions with a rare headed goal. With half an hour to go, they still led 3–0 and all seemed set fair for routine progress into the next round.

So certain were the Newcastle fans of their team's superiority and success that they even began a lighthearted Mexican wave, something that is usually anathema in a real hot-bed of football like St James' Park. The premature celebrations were cut short, however, when a Bilbao substitute, Suances, made one goal and scored another as their English opponents suddenly faded away. The Basque club might even have equalized as Newcastle ended the match holding on like grim death for a 3–2 win. Afterwards, Keegan was honest enough to blame his team's naivety, in trying to increase their lead, for the concession of two away goals that tilted the tie very much in Bilbao's favour.

However, having watched the match at first hand, I'm not so sure naivety was the whole story. It seemed to me that Newcastle had put so much effort into building their 3–0 lead in front of a demanding crowd, they simply ran out of steam in that final half-hour against patient opponents who knew how to manipulate the ball. Whatever the truth of the matter, Keegan's all-or-nothing strategy was suddenly called into question for the first time by the media. Here, it seemed, was substantial proof that you could not conquer Europe with the sort of blitzkrieg that had carried Newcastle so far, so quickly in domestic football.

Yet only the week before the first leg of the tie against Athletic Bilbao, Keegan had again challenged orthodox European tactics with striking success. Invited by the then England coach, Terry

EUROPE AND ANDY

Venables, to stand in for the indisposed Dave Sexton, Keegan took charge of the England Under-21 side and led them to an emphatic European Championship qualifying victory in Austria. Playing at Kapfenberg, a picturesque town in the Austrian Alps, Keegan's England won 3–1, Liverpool's Jamie Redknapp scoring all three, despite going a goal down after only six minutes. But the most revealing thing about the win was Keegan's decision to send on two forwards, Noel Whelan and Nicky Barmby, as his substitutes when England were only 2–1 ahead. It was a risky thing to do, especially as the team was reduced to ten men by the dismissal of Liverpool's Robbie Fowler for dissent a couple of minutes from the end.

It was also a bold step thoroughly typical of Keegan's unusual approach to the game as a manager. Just about every other manager and coach in football would have pulled down the shutters at that point, packed their defence and settled for a narrow and valuable away win. Instead, he sent on two forwards (one of them for midfielder Chris Bart-Williams) and went for another goal. He got it, too, Redknapp lashing home a free-kick almost as soon as Fowler had made the long, lonely walk to the dressing-room. Keegan impressed after the match as well, the command of German he had acquired while a player with Hamburg nearly twenty years earlier enabling him to answer questions fluently in both the relevant languages at the customary press conference. Here, we all thought again, is the England manager-in-waiting.

Nevertheless, the failure to shut up shop and play conservatively against Athletic Bilbao was the major turning point in Newcastle's season. There was no immediate deterioration, it has to be said. Sheffield Wednesday were beaten 2–1 the following Saturday to make it an eleven-game unbeaten start in the League, and Manchester United were knocked out of the Coca-Cola Cup four days later. However, on 29 October, only three days after they had beaten United 2–0 at St James' Park, Newcastle suffered their first defeat of the season by the same score at Old Trafford in the Premiership. Gary Pallister and

THE MAGNIFICENT OBSESSION

Keith Gillespie scored the goals, and Newcastle's capacity for making a telling response was handicapped by the absence of Cole, who was resting his troublesome shins for a month.

Keegan and his players had to go straight from that sickening setback to Bilbao for the second leg of their UEFA tie. Knowing a goalless draw would see them through, they held out stubbornly until a shot from Ciganda was deflected into the net off Steve Howey after sixty-six minutes. That was it, out on the away goals rule again, and there was worse to come. Lacking the injured Cole for four games, Newcastle won only two of their next twelve Premiership matches. Worse still, when Cole did come back in the middle of November, he seemed to have lost the golden touch. After scoring on his return against Ipswich, the deadly marksman of old went ten League and cup games without a goal.

So, in retrospect, it should not have been quite such a great shock when Keegan decided halfway through the season to sell to Manchester United – one of Newcastle's main rivals – the man who had broken most of Newcastle's scoring records. Clearly, the player was becoming rather injury-prone and had stopped scoring goals. Not only that, but hindsight tells us Keegan obviously had other, even better, goalscorers in mind as a replacement. Chris McMenemy hints at that kind of thinking when he says, 'I think there was a long-term plan there. The decision to part with Andy was very brave. The next step for him was to leave this club, and there was only one place to go – Manchester United.' But that is insider-speak for, 'We felt we could afford to let him go.'

There was certainly no residual animosity between Keegan and Cole over the player's disappearance in London and refusal to play in the game at Wimbledon. In fact, they got on very well. 'I remember one instance when Kevin and I were going to watch a game at Liverpool,' says McMenemy. 'It was a wild, wet and windy night and we were just pulling out of the car park at St James' Park when we saw Andy walking in towards the club. All he had on was a leather coat and a pair of jeans.

EUROPE AND ANDY

'We pulled the window down and Kevin said, "Listen, what are you doing tonight?" Andy said he didn't have anything on, so Kevin said, "Come on then, come and see a game of football." He got in the back of the car and we drove through the gale to Liverpool. When we got there, I don't think we had a ticket for Andy, but Kevin is such a legend at Anfield we didn't have any trouble getting him in.

'Kevin went up into a couple of sponsors' lounges, which he needn't have done, and was introduced to people and was very friendly and talked to whoever wanted to talk to him. After the game – I think it was against QPR – we got back in the car, stopped for a cup of coffee and a sandwich at the Tickled Trout (a hotel just off the M6 near Blackburn) and then came all the way back to Newcastle. That was typical Kevin – spur of the moment, what are you doing, come and watch a football match, it's part of your education. And that was how well the two of them got on.

'We talked all the way there and all the way back. It was never a case of the two of them falling out, because they were good for each other. Kevin had brought Andy a long way and, in his own way, Andy had taken Kevin along with him as well. So there wouldn't have been too many closer managers and centre forwards at that particular time, I wouldn't have thought.'

Nevertheless, Keegan clearly felt it was time for Cole to go. The former Newcastle manager may well have explained by now exactly why he decided to sell his leading scorer, but it looks from a distance as though there might have been several reasons for such a momentous decision. One was the shin trouble which had kept Cole out of the side for a month and out of the England squad, another was the gradual drying up of his extraordinary goal-scoring rate – and a third could have been the need to relieve the strain on Newcastle's finances imposed by Keegan's heavy spending on players.

Chris McMenemy hints at more than one of those reasons when he delivers the following eulogy, 'At the time, it [the sale of Cole] was a bombshell for the supporters. A small section of them gathered at the ground that day, and there was the famous scene with Kevin at the top of the stairs and the supporters at the bottom. It was typical of him at the time that he actually went out and faced them and was honest enough to say, "If I get it wrong, I'll be the one that goes, and it'll be judged to have been a mistake." It went on for days and days in the news, but I think it was a brave decision. It was certainly proved to be a good decision in the long run for both parties.

'What people have got to remember is that Andy's time up here was nothing short of phenomenal. He was a modern version of legends like Jackie Milburn and Malcolm Macdonald. It just seemed that every time he went out, you expected him to score – very much like Alan Shearer after him. For a player who had drifted away from Arsenal to Bristol City and then came up here when Newcastle were in the First Division, the progress he made and the value he was to the club should never be underestimated.

'The other thing Andy did very well up here was bridge the racial gap, which has always been endemic in this area. Although they had people like Tony Cunningham here in previous years, Andy was one of the first to really make a huge success of what he did. He had his fair share of problems with racial chants and whatever, but I think he was genuinely loved by the supporters in the end. That was a credit to him as well.

'I think there was a long-term plan there, and Kevin would never shy away from making difficult decisions. All good decisions are decisions made at the right time, and that particular decision, though it didn't seem to the supporters the best time to make it, might have enabled us in the longer term to go for someone like Alan Shearer. The finances that came in and the actual financial state of the club at that time might have had a bearing on whether we sold Andy Cole or kept him. That will come out in time. It certainly was a bombshell – within the club as well as outside it – but in the long term it's proved for Andy and Newcastle one of the best decisions ever made.

'Nobody expected it. After all, he'd scored forty-odd goals

EUROPE AND ANDY

the previous season. Then, all of sudden, to be selling him even for the amount of money we got [£6 million] plus a winger [Keith Gillespie, who was valued at £1 million] was quite a shock. Although you wouldn't wish it on Andy, he had his fair share of injury problems the season after that, and the following season as well. He'd started to get one or two little problems in training here, but I don't think that was part of the decision. It was just a situation that occurred.

'Kevin was genuine enough to think the transfer was probably good for Newcastle United, which was his first priority, and good for Andy Cole. The fact that he'd been a centre forward himself maybe led him to believe Andy had gone as far as he could at Newcastle United. He certainly benefited from playing with Peter Beardsley. He was fortunate to have people like Beardsley and Scott Sellars alongside him. They were very, very good at providing him with the ball.'

It seems the transfer originated in an enquiry Keegan made about Gillespie, a quick, direct winger whom the Newcastle manager valued privately at £2.5 million. Alex Ferguson, the Manchester United manager, responded by asking about the availability of Cole, doubtless doing it in a jocular way that anticipated the usual blunt refusal. So he must almost have fallen off his chair when he was offered some encouragement at the other end of the line. Keegan's unexpected agreement to sell seems to have been another of his famous spur-of-the-moment decisions. The evidence to support that interpretation lies in the efforts Newcastle had been making at the time to find a partner for Cole. But bids submitted to Queen's Park Rangers and Crystal Palace for Les Ferdinand and the Newcastle-born Chris Armstrong respectively had proved unsuccessful.

Although as shocked as everyone else by the idea of selling Cole, the Newcastle board took their usual course and backed Keegan's decision to the hilt. The deal was finalized in Sheffield after Keegan and the two Freddies, Shepherd and Fletcher, had driven down from Newcastle to meet Sir John Hall and put him in the picture. The cover for all this subterfuge was Sheffield

United's FA Cup third round tie against Manchester United at Bramall Lane on a Monday night. Since Newcastle were due to play Manchester United the following weekend, no one questioned why Keegan should be at Bramall Lane for the match.

During the drive down to Sheffield, Keegan had broken the news to Cole on the car phone. The player, too, was taken aback and proved reluctant at first to entertain the idea of leaving Newcastle. But Keegan's silver tongue eventually persuaded Cole a move to Old Trafford would be in his best interests, and the striker agreed to meet Ferguson the following day. Meanwhile, Ferguson informed Gillespie he was willing to let him go to Newcastle as the makeweight in the deal and took the precaution of withdrawing the Northern Ireland international winger from the cup-tie against Sheffield United.

When the news of Cole's transfer to Manchester United hit the streets of Newcastle the following day, it sent the pigeons fluttering into the air with a real squawk. Several hundred angry fans headed straight for St James' Park to register a protest at the sale of the Toon Army's goalscoring hero. What made it worse for them was that the buyers were the club now perceived as Newcastle's greatest rivals in English football, a comparison which was, in itself, a measure of the club's progress during the three years Keegan had been manager. Fears were also expressed that Newcastle, despite all the assurances to the contrary by the new regime, were still basically the selling club who had let outstanding native talent like Peter Beardsley, Chris Waddle and Paul Gascoigne drift away to adorn other clubs.

Typically, Keegan met the trouble head-on. Like one of those sheriffs in a Hollywood western who have to pacify townspeople infuriated by some outrage or other, the Newcastle manager stood at the top of the steps leading up to the main entrance at St James' Park and argued it out with the protesting supporters in the glare of the television lights illuminating the heated little scene. 'If I've got it wrong,' he said in one of the dramatic phrases that came so naturally to him, 'then there's a bullet

EUROPE AND ANDY

with my name on it.' It was pure soap opera, but it did the trick. Keegan's unquestionable bravery in facing the fans, his assurances that he knew how they felt and his guarantee of further signings with the Cole money carried the day. It was a supreme example of not only his indestructible relationship with the Newcastle fans, but his power to bring other people round to his way of thinking.

Even now, John Gibson is still staggered by the success Keegan had in mollifying the fans over the sale of Cole. 'I've always said – and I mean it as a compliment – that Kevin Keegan is the greatest PRO for himself I have ever known,' he says. 'But, because he was so good for himself, he was good for those who employed him as well. He was superb: he could charm the birds out of the trees. Only KK, certainly, could have sold Andy Cole after he had scored forty-one goals for Newcastle and beaten Hughie Gallacher's all-time record, then gone out and met the angry fans and utterly convinced them – after a twenty-minute conversation – that he'd done the right thing! It was quite extraordinary because it was face-to-face. They ended up trusting him to buy a centre forward who would be better than Cole – Newcastle fans who have never trusted a manager in their lives!'

Over the next six months, some of the faithful must have wondered if that trust had been misplaced. There was no sign of a proper replacement for Cole as Newcastle went up from fifth to third place, but slipped back again to finish sixth behind Blackburn, the new champions, Manchester United, Nottingham Forest, Liverpool and Leeds. There was little joy (a 2–0 victory over Manchester United excluded) in the domestic cup competitions, either. Manchester City knocked them out of the Coca-Cola Cup in the fourth round, and Everton beat them in the sixth round of the FA Cup.

Councillor Terry Cooney probably speaks for a lot of Newcastle supporters when he says, 'If Kevin had a problem, he would face it. He certainly did so when they were selling Andy Cole. But that was good business, and there are times when you've got to say, "Right, do I make the move and do it?" The only mistake Kevin made there was that he didn't fill Cole's position as quickly as he should have done. We might have been in a better position if he had. But even he could not be Superman all the time.'

Under the circumstances, it was Paul Kitson who had the misfortune to be regarded as Cole's successor. Chris McMenemy believes the comparison was unfair. 'Paul was the first one to be tried after Andy left,' he says. 'I felt sorry for him because he was a very good footballer and a good lad and it was probably misinterpreted by most of the supporters that he'd come to replace Andy. I don't think that was really the case. Paul was more of a link-up player who obviously had the ability to score goals, but would prefer to come off short for the build-up. Andy, by comparison, was an out-and-out goalscorer, so it was a difficult little cross for Paul to bear. Every time he played, people expected him to go and score goals like Andy Cole, which was never going to be the case.'

Not until Keegan paid Queen's Park Rangers £6 million for Les Ferdinand the following June, in fact, did Newcastle fill the void left by Cole's departure. Perhaps the failure to replace him quickly can be explained to some extent by the fact that Keegan had already spent something like £13 million net on new players in the previous three years and possibly had to rein in his spending for a while. Maybe it just took time to find the right man. But, as the eventful and disappointing 1994–95 season ended without a trophy or a place in Europe, the fans were entitled to wonder whether things might have turned out differently had Cole stayed or a replacement been found sooner.

7

TORMENT

Now came the really big push for the Premiership title Keegan, Newcastle and the fans so craved. In advance of the 1995-96 season, the Newcastle manager went on a shopping spree that made all his previous spending look like small change. In the two months between 7 June and 11 August, Keegan paid out more than £14 million for four new players. They were right full back or wing back Warren Barton (from Wimbledon for £4 million), striker Les Ferdinand (from Queen's Park Rangers for £6 million), left winger David Ginola (from Paris St Germain for £2.5 million) and goalkeeper Shaka Hislop (from Reading for £1.575 million). Those names and figures added up to the clearest possible statement of intent, and the bookies duly made Newcastle favourites again to win the title.

Most of the buys looked good ones at the time. Barton, then twenty-six and one of the many lucky wannabes Wimbledon have snapped up cheaply from non-League football and turned into high-grade footballers, was making such significant progress under Joe Kinnear that England coach Terry Venables had picked him earlier in the year to play against the Republic of Ireland in the ill-fated friendly at Lansdowne Road, which had to be abandoned because English hooligans started smashing the place to pieces. So while that record-breaking £4 million seemed a bit excessive for a defender – any defender but Paolo Maldini or Franco Baresi, in fact – most people were willing to give Keegan the benefit of the doubt for even thinking of strengthening his defence.

There could be no reservations at all about Ferdinand.

Newcastle had needed a suitable replacement for Andy Cole for all of five months, and now here he was. Suitable is hardly the word. At twenty-eight, the quiet, unassuming Londoner could look back on a rather varied career (during which he had been on loan to Brentford and Besiktas of Turkey) knowing he had scored eighty goals in 163 League appearances for QPR – virtually one every two games – and had played seven times for England. Built like a brick outhouse, blessed with fearsome pace and more than a match for anyone in the air, this former non-League footballer looked to be exactly what Newcastle required. That is to say, a bulldozing, high-scoring centre forward in the Jackie Milburn, Malcolm Macdonald tradition.

Needless to say, Newcastle did not get Ferdinand without a fight. After trying for eighteen months to persuade Richard Thompson, QPR's owner and a personal friend of the Halls, to sell his prize asset, Newcastle were nearly pipped at the post by Aston Villa. Having offered £5.5 million for the player, Keegan was forced to match Villa's late bid of £6 million. Fortunately for Newcastle, Ferdinand made it clear that he would rather go to St James' Park than Villa Park, a decision that did not make the fans of the Birmingham club particularly well disposed towards him whenever he played at their ground.

By comparison, the purchase of Ginola was a breeze. Keegan was actually on holiday with his family in Florida when the deal was done at the start of July. Although Arsenal and Celtic were both keen to sign the flamboyant French international, it took only a couple of hours at the seductive Geordie location of the Gosforth Park Hotel, to get him to put his signature on a contract. With injury placing a question mark over the future of Scott Sellars and Newcastle pulling out of the proposed purchase of John Salako, then with Crystal Palace, a left winger was urgently needed. It was quite a coup, therefore, for Keegan to have bought such a celebrated player so cheaply, relatively speaking. No doubt his attention had first been attracted to Ginola by the long-haired player's lively performances for Paris

TORMENT

St Germain against Arsenal in the European Cup-Winners' Cup a couple of seasons earlier.

It is said that signing Ginola was Keegan's response to losing out on Roberto Baggio, then still with Juventus. Alan Oliver, who ran the story about the Baggio bid in the *Evening Chronicle* for two days with little response from a sceptical national press, insists Newcastle were prepared to pay Juventus all of £9 million for the little pony-tailed hobgoblin, at that time the most famous and talented player in Italy. According to Oliver, Newcastle even beefed up their usual delegation of Douglas Hall and the two Freddies with Terry McDermott and the owner of an Italian restaurant in Newcastle, who acted as their interpreter. It was all a bit farcical, in that no one from Juventus was prepared to meet them and they had to do their negotiating through an agent. In the end, the deal broke down, allegedly, because Baggio wanted £64,000 a week, which was beyond the pocket of even Sir John Hall and his free-spending Newcastle United.

Rather more down-to-earth was the signing of goalkeeper Shaka Hislop from First Division Reading for a little over £1.5 million just a week before the start of the 1995–96 season. But it was routine only so far as the fee and the selling club were concerned. Hislop himself had had anything but a mundane life and career before ending up at St James' Park. Born in Hackney, in the East End of London, he moved to Trinidad with his parents when he was two. Then, as a West Indian teenager more interested in soccer than cricket, he was awarded a four-year scholarship at Howard University in Washington, DC, where he graduated in mechanical engineering. His professional career began with the American indoor club Baltimore Blast, from whom Reading eventually signed him in 1992. Over the next three years, Hislop made 126 appearances for Reading and earned a reputation for being the best goalkeeper outside the Premiership.

The signing was practical in that Pavel Srnicek, Newcastle's first-choice goalkeeper, was suspended for the first two games of the new season. But there was also a feeling that Keegan's team needed a keeper more reliable than the often inspired but occasionally fallible Czech Republic international. In the event, Srnicek did not have much say in the argument during the first half of the season. Having gone straight into the side, Hislop kept his place until he was injured in the 1–0 defeat at Chelsea on 9 December.

By then Newcastle had firmly established themselves as leaders of the Premiership. Even though Keegan's team, along with several other clubs, continued to find that trips to play Wimbledon were usually unrewarding, the 3–3 draw they got against the London club on 3 December meant they were five points clear of Manchester United at the top. It was hardly surprising, since Newcastle had won all but three of their first fifteen League matches. Outstanding among those early results was a 6–1 hammering of Wimbledon at St James' Park, an unusually heavy defeat for a team everyone finds hard to beat. Ferdinand scored a hat-trick in that game, taking his total for the first ten games to a remarkable thirteen goals.

There was a slight hiccup on 9 December, when Newcastle lost 1–0 at Chelsea and suffered only their second defeat of the season. But successive home wins against Everton and Nottingham Forest put them in good heart for the acid test at Old Trafford two days after Christmas. They must have been encouraged, too, by the knowledge that Manchester United had lost their previous two matches, away to Liverpool and Leeds. Yet, when it came to the crunch, Newcastle folded again. Goals from Andy Cole, of all people, and Roy Keane enabled the dominant club in English football to extend their unbeaten run against Keegan's ambitious team. Like *Private Eye*'s Ron Knee, the Newcastle manager was ashen-faced. 'The circus came to town, but we came without the lions and tigers,' Keegan told the press afterwards, reeling off yet another of the aphorisms that had become his stock-in-trade.

In truth, however, losing at Old Trafford was just a temporary interruption to Newcastle's seemingly unstoppable march

Kevin Keegan scores on his debut for Newcastle, against Queens Park Rangers in 1982. The start of his enduring love affair with the Toon Army.

Sir John Hall, the man whose money enabled Keegan to revitalize Newcastle United.

An aerial view of Wynard Hall, Sir John Hall's now famous stately home.

Sir John and Douglas Hall pulling off their daring coup at the press conference called to present Keegan as the new manager of Newcastle United.

Keegan and Sir John Hall united by United – the way it was for most of the five years prior to their falling out.

Above: Keegan and McDermott salute the fans at St James' Park after the 7–1 win against Leicester that celebrated Newcastle's elevation into the Premier League as First Division champions in 1993.

Left: Later in the partnership, the strain begins to show.

One of the indelible images of Keegan's reign. He attacks Manchester United manager Alex Ferguson in that infamous TV interview.

Keegan at his most persuasive – he pacifies a crowd of angry Newcastle fans after selling their hero, Andy Cole.

With the weight of Geordie expectations on his shoulders, Keegan in pensive mood during a game against Manchester United.

Tension shows as caretaker manager Terry McDermott and defensive coach Mark Lawrenson continue the battle after Keegan's departure.

Peter Beardsley, possibly Keegan's favourite player – the man who did as much as anybody to turn Newcastle's fortunes around.

The players on whose transfers most of the £60 million was spent...

Les Ferdinand

Alan Shearer

David Batty

David Ginola

Tino Asprilla

TORMENT

towards the title and success in the Coca-Cola Cup. Five consecutive Premiership victories followed the defeat by Manchester United and wins against Bristol City, Stoke City and Liverpool had taken Newcastle into the fifth round of the cup competition. Things were going pretty swimmingly, therefore, until Newcastle went to Highbury for their fifth-round Coca-Cola Cup tie against Arsenal on 10 January. They lost 2–0, but it is probably remembered better as the game in which Ginola was sent off for elbowing former England international right back Lee Dixon in the face. The Frenchman exacted his own retribution after receiving some rough treatment from Dixon, an old adversary from the time Arsenal had played Paris St Germain in the Cup-Winners' Cup, and the Gunners' other full back, Nigel Winterburn. In fact, Winterburn might have been sent off for one tackle on Ginola, whose not undeserved reputation for 'diving' was probably responsible, to some extent, for the referee's lack of sympathy and failure to give him adequate protection.

Keegan was so incensed by what had happened to his precious new signing that he became embroiled in yet another touchline fracas, this time with Bruce Rioch, the Arsenal manager and an equally volatile character. In the end, the police had to move in to restore order as Terry McDermott joined the fray. It was not a very edifying scene and it was not, of course, the first time Keegan had allowed his emotions to get the better of him in the heat of battle. All of a sudden, the Newcastle manager's suspect temperament was a hot issue again.

The feeling that mischievous gods might be beginning to toy with Keegan and Newcastle was strengthened a week later, when they were knocked out of the FA Cup as well. Worst of all, they were beaten at home on penalties in a third-round replay against Chelsea. With Ginola facing a three-match suspension for his indiscretion at Highbury, it hardly helped, either, that Darren Peacock was sent off by Barnsley referee Steve Lodge during the replay.

Yet, dismissal from both the domestic cup competitions looked as though it could be a blessing in disguise. Not having qualified for Europe, either, Newcastle were left completely free to concentrate exclusively on their major priority, becoming champions of England for the first time since 1926–27. They were in pole position, too, their 2–1 home win against Bolton on Saturday 20 January – three days after being knocked out of the FA Cup – taking them twelve points clear of Liverpool and Manchester United. It was something of an exaggerated lead, in that it lasted only until the following Monday, when Manchester United's crucial 1–0 win at West Ham, courtesy of another of Eric Cantona's priceless goals for the club, reduced it to nine points. Even so, most clubs would have been more than glad to have so much daylight between themselves and the chasing pack going into the final fifteen games of the season.

Not only that, but Keegan's response to the cup setbacks was typically positive and typically extravagant. In the next couple of months, he went out and paid more than eleven million in all for the Colombian international striker Faustino Asprilla and the England midfielder David Batty. He also tried to sign his old mate Chris Waddle and the quicksilver Swedish winger Jesper Blomqvist, but both deals fell through. However, in terms of star names, Asprilla and Batty were not bad to be going on with. Asprilla, certainly, was one of the most exotic figures ever to pull on the famous black-and-white-striped shirt. He was not the first South American to do that: George Robledo and Mirandinha, to name but two, had beaten him to it. Nevertheless, few players can have come to St James' Park trailing the sort of lurid reputation the Colombian brought as excess luggage.

As Alan Oliver put it incredulously in *Geordie Messiah*, '... the tabloids had a field day with Asprilla. Guns, drugs, bar brawls, porn queens. And that was on a quiet day.' There were so many stories about Asprilla's allegedly wild behaviour off the field, it was not unreasonable to conclude that here was a man who enjoyed living life to the full. That predilection has often gone hand-in-hand with an unusual ability to manipulate a football, and there could not be any doubt that Asprilla was extravagantly gifted in the latter respect.

TORMENT

Nicknamed the 'Octopus' in his youth because of an almost double-jointed capacity for claiming the ball with his long, sinuous legs, Asprilla had established himself in Europe with the up-and-coming Italian club Parma. He was a member of their side that won the European Cup-Winners' Cup in 1993 (though he missed the final against Antwerp at Wembley) and played against Arsenal in the final when the London club won the same competition the following year.

Batty joined the Newcastle squad from Blackburn a month after Asprilla. He agreed to sign for them on the day the Colombian played his third game for the club, a fractious 3–3 draw with Manchester City at Maine Road during which Asprilla clashed infamously with City defender Keith Curle. The stocky Yorkshireman could hardly have chosen a more important match in which to make his own debut. It was the return Premiership game against Manchester United at St James' Park on 4 March in which Newcastle could have gone seven points clear of their opponents or seen their lead cut to one. This time, Keegan's team threatened to play their great rivals off the park, only to be thwarted by the brilliance of the Danish international goalkeeper Peter Schmeichel and then beaten by one of the seven goals Cantona scored in his club's last ten games that season.

At twenty-seven, Batty had played seventeen times for England and gained a reputation, with Leeds United, his first club, and Blackburn, for being an aggressive midfield ball-winner in the Nobby Stiles mould. He had also shown he could pass the ball accurately, but so much of his work at that stage was negative in nature that he was seen as no more than someone who could stiffen the Newcastle midfield with some much-needed steel. Indeed, the imbalance then in Batty's game between destructiveness and creativity was probably responsible for Terry Venables' decision to omit him from the England squad for Euro '96.

However, Keegan obviously saw Batty as a better all-round proposition than Lee Clark, a then shaven-headed local lad who had given his all for the club during the fight to avoid relegation to the old Third Division and the climb towards the pinnacle of English football. Clark was talented enough himself to have won eleven England Under-21 caps, but he and Keith Gillespie were the players who had to make way for the introduction of Batty and Asprilla respectively, the expensive newcomers the forward-thinking Newcastle manager clearly believed would guarantee the club their first League Championship for sixty-nine years. Instead, the whole thing began to unravel.

There had been a nice balance to the team at that time, despite the absence of Albert, who missed most of the first half of the season due to injury. Howey proved an able deputy for the Belgian international in the centre of the back-four, alongside Peacock, while the blond Barton and the then peroxided Beresford complemented each other nicely at full back. Similarly, in midfield, the pace of Gillespie on one flank and the trickery and high-powered shooting of Ginola on the other were underpinned by the industry and enterprise of Lee and Clark in between. Then, up front, the guile of Beardsley was the perfect counterpoint to the battering-ram qualities of Ferdinand.

Now, with Asprilla up alongside Ferdinand, Beardsley in attack and Gillespie watching from the bench, Newcastle looked poorer for the lack of someone to beat a man on the right and deliver crosses Ferdinand could put away with his head. To be fair, Asprilla engineered an unlikely victory on his debut against Middlesbrough and scored three goals after that. But despite the manful attempts of Lee and Beardsley to make good the deficiency, Newcastle lost the width on the right that had served them so well. They also lost the attacking brio that Clark had brought to his midfield duties. Batty has developed the scope of his game enormously since joining Newcastle, but at that point he was a seriously negative influence without significantly increasing Newcastle's defensive soundness.

Without much doubt, the 2–0 defeat at West Ham on 21 February was the real turning-point. Newcastle won only five of the twelve games which remained after that, and their awesome, apparently unassailable, twelve-point lead dwindled to nothing. Their four costly losses included a crucial 1–0 home defeat by Manchester United – Cantona scoring the winner yet again – and an absolutely shattering outcome to a match at Liverpool on 3 April that everyone acknowledged to be the most thrilling game of the season, if not the century. The advantage swung one way, then the other, as the teams scored three goals apiece. An honourable draw seemed certain until Liverpool's Stan Collymore materialized at the far post in injury-time to drive the ball into the net and the Newcastle fans to distraction.

For many of us, the abiding memory of the 1995–96 season will always be those television close-ups of distraught men, women and children in black and white stripes scarcely able to believe the evidence in front of their own eyes as their team's big lead at the top of the Premiership slowly evaporated away to nothing. Even after the sickening defeat at Liverpool and another at Blackburn, Newcastle were not quite done for – as successive wins against Aston Villa, Southampton and Leeds proved – but they knew in their heart of hearts they had no chance of holding off a rampant, experienced Manchester United team, who won all but two of their final fifteen Premiership matches in a devastating sprint for the finishing line.

Steve Wraith, editor of the *No. 9* fanzine, conveys some of the agony the Newcastle supporters were going through when he says, 'Playing well and not winning anything did begin to grate on the fans the season we gave the title to Manchester United. There were so many great Newcastle United fans travelling to away games, they deserved some reward. But I think we knew the team weren't going to win the title when we lost 2–1 at Blackburn. We thought we were going to do it when David Batty put us 1–0 up. Then those two goals [by Blackburn's Geordie striker Graham Fenton in the last five minutes] went in and, quite honestly, it gutted me. That was it: I knew then we were not going to win the title.

'Although it was still mathematically possible to do it – it could go to the last game of the season and all that – it drained me, that day. What made it worse was to go back and watch it on a video recorder and see Sky revelling in the fact that Newcastle United fans were suffering and the club were under-achieving. They'd put all this money into the club and, again, nothing was going to come of it. It was heart-breaking and I think we knew something had to be done.'

Keegan's own frustration at letting it all slip away had been obvious in his dejected body language at Anfield. And it now culminated in a memorable outburst on television – and a defining moment in this story – following Newcastle's 1–0 win at Leeds on 29 April. Manchester United had struggled to beat the Yorkshire club by the same score at home twelve days earlier and their manager, Alex Ferguson, had been moved to criticize the Leeds players for what he saw as their failure to play as competitively as that more often for their manager, the beleaguered Howard Wilkinson, a good friend of his.

Keegan, however, interpreted Ferguson's remarks as a deliberate and unethical attempt to gee the Leeds players up for their next match – at home to Newcastle. He also saw them as part of a verbal campaign by the Manchester United manager to undermine Newcastle's title bid. So he could not contain his anger while being interviewed at the end of Sky's coverage of the game at Elland Road. 'The battle is still on,' he ranted. 'Manchester United haven't won this yet. Alex Ferguson has still got to go to Middlesbrough and get something. We are still fighting for this title and I'd love it, just love it, if we beat them. A lot of things have been said over the past few weeks – a lot of it slanderous. You have got to send Alex Ferguson a tape of this game. That's what he wanted, isn't it?'

As far as the Toon Army were concerned, Keegan's explosion of feeling was up there on a par with Henry V's pre-match team talk at Agincourt. The manager had said exactly what the Newcastle footsoldiers themselves would have liked to say publicly, given the chance. Most other people took a markedly different view, however. To them, Keegan looked a man at the end of his tether, a man who had lost control of the situation and of himself. A man, too, who had allowed himself to be wound up by the mind-games Ferguson is fond of playing with other managers. Not that in this case there was any *prima facie* evidence of an ulterior motive in his criticism of the Leeds players.

Sure enough, the night before Newcastle's final Premiership fixture of the season, a home game against Tottenham (now managed by Gerry Francis, not Ossie Ardiles), Keegan offered his resignation to the board of directors. They persuaded him to change his mind, but here was the first clear sign that he was no longer happy in the job. It was as though he felt he had let everyone down, a feeling not improved by Newcastle's failure to beat Spurs and the news of Manchester United's clinching, 3–0 victory at Middlesbrough. The Old Trafford club were champions again, reclaiming the Premiership title they had won in the new league's first two seasons and then lost to Blackburn. After being those twelve points behind with less than half the season remaining, they finished four points ahead of Newcastle in the end.

Not to have won the title after being in such a strong position to end the club's long wait for it must have been a shattering experience for everyone at St James' Park. Chris McMenemy gives some idea of what it was like to be on the inside of that high-pressure situation as Manchester United slowly closed the gap and then overtook Newcastle. 'The club had never been in first place before, so it was completely new to just about everybody,' he points out. 'I don't think there was a player in the squad, with the exception of Peter Beardsley, who had been part of a title-winning team. Obviously Kevin and Terry had won the League before as players, but that was before it became the Premier League. So the longer it went on, you found yourself thinking it was tremendous to be in that position, but you were always looking over your shoulder and asking, "Are you really big enough for this position? Do you know how to handle it?"

'We went to West Ham when we still had a big lead, and we should have won. We dominated most of the game, but they scored early and very late. In between their goals, and even before the first one, we'd really played well and deserved to win. But we didn't, and when we went into the dressing-room, Kevin said something to the effect that, "Well, that was the one to win!" He'd said it before the game, he said it afterwards and he was right. Because, after that, it seemed that whenever we played on a Monday night, Manchester United played on the Sunday. So, all the time, the pressure was building on us. Everybody made a great hoo-ha about Kevin's reaction after the Leeds game, but no one mentions that it was a great result for us and a decent performance. In the end, though, Manchester United just kept winning and winning while we drew one, or had a gap and then won a couple.

'It was terrible for the supporters, yet they still wanted us to do a lap of honour at the end of the season because we'd come second. And when you put it all into perspective, which you had to, you realized they were delighted because Newcastle hadn't finished that high in the top division of English football since the war. Even so, you felt for the fans because they'd put so much into it. You also felt for the players, who'd got so close. Especially the local lads who'd been here when they had nothing and had had the chance to become part of history.

'It was a tremendous team effort to have got in a position to win the title, but we hadn't won it and as we are professionals there was a little bit of pain in there for us. The chairman came in and said, "We are ahead of schedule and didn't think we'd have got this far by now," but, deep down, he knew that was the time to win it. It's a terrible feeling, but one that you use or let it affect you. The structure was there to go on and challenge again, which we have done.'

So far as Keegan was concerned, the great chance had been missed. He knew better than anyone that Newcastle should have grabbed their golden opportunity to become the champions of England again after such a long wait and it clearly depressed him that they hadn't. Therefore, it became a question of trying again or not trying at all.

8

THE APOCALYPSE

It was news that really did rock the world of football – and much of the world outside it, too. The verb to rock has been seriously devalued by over-use in the tabloids, but the announcement on 30 July 1996 that Newcastle had paid a then world record fee of £15 million for Alan Shearer did send genuine shock-waves rippling through the round-ball community across the globe. People were taken aback for all sorts of reasons. Not least among those was disbelief that Newcastle could muster such a colossal fee after four years of unusually heavy spending. Indeed, Tottenham chairman Alan Sugar dismissed the idea of laying out so much money on one player as economic madness. Elsewhere in the world, there was astonishment that the English were now capable of outdoing the acknowledged big spenders of world football, the Italians, when it came to buying players.

If nothing else, the Shearer transfer fee, which was £2 million greater than the one AC Milan had paid Torino for Gianluigi Lentini four years earlier and not far off *double* the British record of £8.5 million it cost Liverpool to sign Stan Collymore from Nottingham Forest in 1995, stands as a significant milestone in the rapid development of the Premier League. It showed just how much wealth was now accessible to the twenty members of English football's elite group, mainly through the £304 million, five-year deal they had struck jointly with BSkyB and BBC Television in 1992, and it sent out 'welcome' signals to even more of the world's best players.

As for Keegan and Newcastle, the signing appeared at the time to be a typically spirited reaction by the feisty little manager to missing out on the Premiership title so heart-breakingly the season before. 'All right,' he seemed to be saying to Manchester United, 'you may have beaten us last season, but we're out to get you this time.' Keegan had already chalked up one victory over Alex Ferguson, of course, by persuading Shearer to join Newcastle instead of Manchester United, with whom Shearer had had serious discussions, or Juventus, with whom he did not pursue negotiations. In the player's mind it was clearly a straight choice between joining the English champions and all that implied, or returning to his first love, Newcastle United.

That Shearer is a Geordie who grew up supporting Newcastle United was obviously a major factor in his final choice – he said as much a week after the staggering deal was done, on the day he was paraded in front of the world's press and thousands of delighted fans at St James' Park. Here he was, one of the thousands who had queued up to see Kevin Keegan make his debut for the club as a player in 1982 and a ball-boy on the night the great Tyneside god was wafted away into the skies by helicopter two years later, coming home to make his club great again.

The £15 million question, of course, has to be why Newcastle did not sign the teenage Shearer for nothing while they had the chance. The easy answer is that Jack Hixon, the celebrated North East scout who discovered him playing for Cramlington Juniors, was working for Southampton at the time. However, considering that Shearer spent five days with Newcastle on trial before signing associated schoolboy forms with Southampton in 1984, one cannot help but think a mistake must have been made somewhere along the line. Whichever way you look at it, the failure to keep Shearer at St James' Park – his spiritual home – as a boy appears to have been just another example of Newcastle's strange reluctance, or inability, during that fallow period in the club's history to harvest the region's abundant talent.

To be fair, the signing in 1996 was not Newcastle's first attempt to rectify their mistake – if mistake it had been. Back in the summer of 1992, at the time when Shearer decided he

THE APOCALYPSE

needed to move on from Southampton to further his career, Keegan was looking to strengthen his side, having kept them out of the former Third Division. Shearer was an obvious target, but Newcastle's efforts to speak to him or put in a bid were vetoed by Ian Branfoot, who was at that time the Southampton manager. According to Branfoot, himself a Geordie, a deal had already been done with Blackburn and no matter how much Keegan and Sir John Hall offered, it would be topped by Kenny Dalglish and Jack Walker. So, for a then British record fee of £3.3 million, Shearer went to the team of League champions generous Jack was building in his unfashionable home town.

However, by persuading Shearer to return to his roots, Keegan almost certainly did the leading clubs in the Premier League a favour. Had this outstanding player – the deadliest striker of his generation – joined Manchester United, it is unlikely that anyone would have been able to challenge the supremacy in English football they had established under the astute management of Alex Ferguson. In other words, Shearer's move from Blackburn Rovers to Newcastle United gave everyone else a chance. It is said, of course, that Shearer's freedom of choice was somewhat limited by Blackburn's reluctance to sell their most potent weapon to their most hated rivals. Whatever his reason for choosing Newcastle United, it meant Shearer had turned down Manchester United for a second time; because they, too, had wanted him when he was leaving Southampton. And spurning England's most successful club twice takes some doing.

There is no doubt that what Newcastle were getting for their mountain of money was somebody very special. Shearer's goalscoring record spoke for itself: only twenty-three in 118 League appearances when he was learning his trade with Southampton; but an incredible 112 in 138 for Blackburn. On top of that were the five goals which had made Shearer top scorer in the finals of Euro '96, in which England reached the semi-finals and were unlucky not to go further. Shearer's supremacy in that tournament followed a barren spell for his country long enough to have made some strikers curl up and die. So Newcastle had bought a player who was not only a striker of immense talent but also a mature human being with an unflappable temperament and great strength of character. As David Platt, Shearer's England room-mate, once said of him, 'He's the oldest twenty-three-year-old I've ever met!'

When he joined them, Newcastle's latest and most expensive acquisition was just a fortnight away from his twenty-sixth birthday and at the height of his powers. Keegan shone with delighted anticipation as he described how Shearer and Ferdinand, in tandem, were going to terrorize opposing defences. It was certainly quite a prospect – two powerful and lethal England strikers operating alongside each other at club level. It looked a winning combination on paper, but it remained to be seen whether it would work in practice. Were Shearer and Ferdinand not a little too similar in style, perhaps? At a time when England coach Terry Venables had just shown in Euro '96 – using Shearer and Teddy Sheringham – that split strikers could be very effective at the highest level of competition, was this not a step backwards?

That the answer to those questions was in the negative, so far as Premiership football was concerned, became evident pretty quickly. Shearer and Ferdinand scored seven times each in Newcastle's first ten games of the 1996–97 season, eight of which were won. They also claimed another four between them as Halmstad and Ferencvaros were brushed aside in the UEFA Cup. Their fusillade of goals reached a rousing climax in the 5–0 hammering Newcastle gave the team they had never seemed able to beat, Manchester United, at St James' Park on 20 October. Shearer and Ferdinand got one apiece in a memorable victory that more than made up for the 4–0 mauling the champions and FA Cup winners had given Newcastle in the Charity Shield match at Wembley just a couple of months earlier.

Keegan's team were back on top of the table, but trouble was waiting just around the corner. Four days after the destruction of Manchester United, it was announced that Shearer had to have an operation on his groin which was scheduled to keep him

THE APOCALYPSE

out of action for up to eight weeks. In the event, this amazingly quick healer came back after only a month; even so, it was a long time for Newcastle to be without a player expected to make the difference between finishing second and first in the Premiership. The initial news hardly improved Keegan's mood, which had not been good from the moment his team had been humiliated at Wembley by Manchester United.

Keegan had taken that particular defeat very badly. He was angered so much by the way his players had, as he saw it, capitulated too easily that he tore them off a strip for half an hour in a locked dressing-room afterwards. The atmosphere did not improve when Newcastle lost their opening Premiership game at Everton 2–0 and were beaten at home 2–1 by Sheffield Wednesday in the third match of the season. Keegan 'gagged' his players after the defeat at Goodison Park, something he had rarely done before, and then lambasted them again for losing to Sheffield Wednesday. When Newcastle responded to that poor start – and their manager's tongue-lashings – by launching a run of seven consecutive victories by beating arch-rivals Sunderland at Roker Park, Keegan chided the press for their criticism before storming out . . . Yet no one had criticized his team more than he had. Clearly, he was not a happy bunny.

Shearer's three-match absence from the team at the end of October and the beginning of November saw Newcastle's form go into a steep decline that had dragged them down to sixth place by Christmas. Of the nine matches they played between the thrashing of Manchester United on 20 October and the Boxing Day fixture, only one was won and four were lost. The last two defeats in that bad run, at Coventry and Blackburn on 17 and 26 December respectively, were the point of no return for Keegan as manager of Newcastle United. At Highfield Road, where Coventry won 2–1, with one goal scored by Darren Huckerby – sold by Newcastle only a month earlier – and another made by him, a stony-faced Keegan chose not to attend the obligatory post-match press conference. In the dressing-room at Ewood Park, after Kevin Gallacher had scored a late winner for the home side, he tore into his players more fiercely than ever before.

He really was nearing the end of his tether now, and the day after the Blackburn defeat Keegan told the Newcastle directors for a second time that he wanted to quit; but again they talked him out of it. The day after that, a Saturday, Newcastle were at home to a Tottenham team severely weakened by injuries to key players. Keegan's team ran riot, Shearer, Ferdinand and Robert Lee scoring two goals each in a 7–1 win. The Newcastle manager, however, took no pleasure from the thumping victory. Saying he had to rush home because his wife, Jean, was ill, Keegan sent Terry McDermott in to face the press – a job he would have normally relished in such circumstances.

'Kevin had talked privately to the directors about quitting on at least three previous occasions,' claims John Gibson, 'and they'd pulled him back from the brink. The most notable case was towards the end of the season, when it was apparent Newcastle were going to blow their twelve-point lead. After they had played QPR, he told the board privately that he was going to quit at the end of the season. I think there were about four games to go. Then, right at the death, on the eve of the last game against Spurs, they pulled him back from the brink again and got him to stay on.

'He came out before the Spurs game and denied he was leaving, but he was denying a story that hadn't been run. Everybody knew he was thinking about it, though. But, at the end of the season, there was the summer's rest and he stayed on. I wonder, with hindsight, whether it wouldn't have been better for Newcastle to have accepted the inevitable then, because I think that the directors believed they were sitting on a time-bomb.'

The outward signs of Keegan's unhappiness had by this time become so obvious that the fans began to sense something was wrong and the city of Newcastle was buzzing with rumours that the manager had been talked out of resigning by the board. The conjecture came to a head on Sunday 5 January 1997, when Brian McNally of the *Sunday Mirror* ran a story suggesting

THE APOCALYPSE

Keegan was thinking of quitting. It was the day Newcastle were in south London for a televised FA Cup third-round tie with Charlton, and Keegan seemed more like his old self when he attended the press conference after the 1–1 draw – until he was asked about the *Sunday Mirror* story, that is. Having failed to sidestep the question, he said dismissively, 'You know the guy who wrote it. End of story!' before turning angrily on his heel. As it happens, McNally is an award-winning sports writer and the departing Keegan was jeered by the press corps with whom he used to have such a cordial relationship. It was a sad way to end a gloriously open era.

There was silence at St James' Park for a couple of days after that. Then, on Wednesday 8 January came the official announcement that Kevin Keegan had resigned as manager of Newcastle United. In *Geordie Messiah*, Alan Oliver describes the reaction as follows, 'The atmosphere in Newcastle was sombre. It was unreal. Fans said they felt as though there had been a death in the family . . . The tributes flowed in . . . Every one was genuine. Some were sad. Some were even funny. The wittiest undoubtedly came from the supporter who said, "To see someone else in charge of Newcastle United will be like watching wor lass [my wife] in bed with another bloke."'

There have been less sympathetic reactions from the fans since the initial shock of Keegan's departure has receded. Though they still revere him for putting Newcastle back among England's leading clubs, some felt betrayed by his and the club's failure at the time to fully explain the reasons for his resignation. Steve Wraith, editor of the fanzine *No. 9*, said, 'Kevin did betray the fans, because there was no explanation. There was just a statement handed out on the day; bye. The directors of the club, Douglas Hall in particular, whose name was on the statement, and Graham Courtney [Newcastle United's press officer] were left to carry the can and stand out front and talk about it.

'It left a lot of disillusioned Newcastle United supporters, who thought there was a chance of getting Kevin back, outside the ground crying. I think on the day, like, it was seen as betrayal.

But they didn't know who to direct their anger at. Whether to direct it at the board, whether to direct it at Kevin or whether to direct it at the players, because it was an abysmal game they played at Blackburn Rovers that day when, reportedly, Kevin spat the dummy and walked out. But although I do feel betrayed, I can't really speak for the rest of the Newcastle United fans. I make a point of never being a spokesman for them: I've only got my own view.

'Like most Newcastle United fans, I'll always remember him as the Messiah; but there's a bitter after-taste in my mouth because I wonder why he left. There are some nasty rumours flying around which you can't publish. Those kind of rumours don't do Kevin's credibility any good. But if he had come out on a podium, even in Southampton or Florida or wherever he was at the time, and said, "All right, I'll call a press conference. Just get it out the way," that would have been great as far as the fans are concerned. But there's still this thing in the mind, you know, that why didn't he tell us the truth on the day? There'll be more Newcastle fans who will lose a bit of respect for him if the story comes out in his book. The way you sell a book is to have an exclusive in it. And this book's going to have to have some interesting stories and revelations in it to sell it.'

The book to which Wraith refers is, of course, the Keegan autobiography, which was due to be published in advance of this more objective view of the period. Just about everyone on Tyneside was waiting for it to appear. Some with trepidation, but most with a simple sense of curiosity about what exactly it was that prompted Keegan to walk away from the club and the supporters with whom he had formed such a close emotional bond. He had thrown out a few hints here and there, but nothing very convincing. These included a claim that he was upset by the anguish Gerry Francis, the Tottenham manager and a former England team-mate, suffered when Newcastle hammered Spurs 7–1 at the end of December 1996.

'I think it's a bit annoying that Kevin tried to blame it [his resignation] on Gerry Francis,' adds Wraith. 'We know he works

THE APOCALYPSE

for a certain tabloid newspaper [the *Sun*], and they've obviously said they want an exclusive. So he's turned round and blamed it on Francis. He says he didn't like doing that to his old mate and that was the time he knew he had to get out of the game. Then on TV, when he was caught unawares at the races, Kevin had to make up another story and say he couldn't take the pressure any more. It had got on top of him and, as far as he was concerned, he had to leave.'

Keegan's most revealing comments, in advance of his autobiography, came in a live television show in South Africa hosted by the former Manchester United and England goalkeeper Gary Bailey. Replying to viewers' questions, Keegan claimed that Newcastle's flotation on the Stock Exchange had had a major bearing on his decision. His willingness to continue as manager only until the end of the 1996–97 season, he suggested, was simply not acceptable to a club preparing a prospectus for the City. They needed him to sign the new, two-year contract they were offering so that investors could be guaranteed stability and continuity. He also claimed he was told he had to raise £6 million by selling players and confessed that he did not think he was getting through to his squad towards the end.

There is some corroboration for all of those points. Let us take the last one first. Mark Lawrenson, the former Liverpool and Republic of Ireland defender Keegan recruited as a defensive coach in October 1996, was actually present when the balloon went up at Blackburn on Boxing Day. 'Kevin came in afterwards, spoke to the players and was very down,' recalls Lawrenson. 'I was standing with Terry McDermott and he came over to us and went, "That's it! They are not listening to me," and just disappeared out the door. Then we heard he'd gone.

'I don't know who it was – Douglas Hall or Freddie Shepherd – but they said he said, "I'll go now." I don't think they could do any more. They had sat him down and said, "Hold on a minute! You've only lost a game." But I think he'd sown the seed then. I believe he said he'd stay on until the end of the season and was told he couldn't do that because of the flotation. One of the great problems with the flotation was they had to know that somebody was going to be involved on a long-term basis. That was Kevin's major problem: he didn't really want to commit himself to that.'

John Gibson thinks it very likely that the Newcastle players had stopped listening to Keegan, as he had claimed after the Coventry game. 'I always remember Jack Charlton saying to me that he would never stay at a club more than four years,' reflects the local newspaperman. 'He said that players, however great they are, will respond to you for a time but, in due course, they are just hearing the same thing over and over again and you lose them. And I believe that Kevin had unquestionably lost the dressing-room. I don't mean they didn't want to play for him, it was just that the edge was gone.

'I think footballers are basically like sheep. If they see a worried, depressed leader, they begin to doubt themselves. And Kevin was always so positive that people would follow him through brick walls. He'd say, in effect, "We'll be all right, kids. The wall will break and we'll get through." But when you see him doubting the brick wall as his opponent, then players doubt it as well.'

The real damage to Keegan's durability had been done the previous season, Lawrenson believes, when that twelve-point lead was squandered. 'I think not winning the title in those circumstances knocked the stuffing out of him,' he opines. 'I also think he honestly thought the players he'd brought in had got to the stage where they weren't listening to him any more. So he thought to himself, "What do you do?" You either change the players you've brought in – and that's going to take some time – or you say, "Right, I'm not enjoying this. I've had five great years. Thanks very much, but no thanks very much." '

John Gibson agrees. 'My honest opinion, after being very close to the man through working with him for a long time,' he says, 'was that when Newcastle didn't win the title after having a twelve-point lead, it dawned on him that the dream would never happen. I think he believed that was his season

THE APOCALYPSE

and he was about to do it. He gave it another shot, which wasn't quite half-hearted, but wasn't with the wild enthusiasm he'd had before. If you fall off Everest three-quarters of the way up, do you want to try to scale it again three months later? It becomes almost impossible to do.

'It killed him, not winning the title from that position of strength. I don't think he could really believe it had happened to him. But it did happen, and he knew his chance was gone. From then on it was just a matter of when he would go. Everybody – the Newcastle board, who believed in him so passionately, as did the fans and as did the press, in truth, because he was bringing success to an area that hadn't had success for an awful long time – began to ask "When?"'

Neither Gibson nor Lawrenson was really surprised when Keegan decided to quit. The physical evidence of stress was there for all to see in the greying of that trademark mane of jet-black hair and the lining of his once boyish face. But those closer to him had noticed signs of psychological deterioration as well. 'Training was always very important to Kevin,' says Lawrenson. 'He trained every day: very rarely did he miss a session. He liked the banter and I think he was at his most comfortable with the players. He enjoyed the mickey-taking, he enjoyed being part of the working hard because he worked very hard in training as well.

'But when he left, you could see he had lost all his natural enthusiasm. Whatever Kevin does, he's naturally enthusiastic about it. You know, if someone said to him, "C'mon gaffer, let's go play wallyball!" he'd say, "Oh yeah! I need a fiver. I'll take some money off you lot." But he'd lost all that. You could see from his training that it had become a chore for him.'

Chris McMenemy however, begs to differ slightly. 'I'm not sure Kevin had lost his enthusiasm,' he says. 'He always had enthusiasm for anything he did. He would come in of a morning and want a game of squash or head tennis or five-a-side. He was always competitive. He didn't lose that, but what I think he did lose was a little bit of sparkle that he'd always had. If you went in in the morning, he'd light the place up. That sort of waned a bit.

'I don't think it had left him: he just needed a boost to charge him up, because he was carrying everybody. He was carrying the whole city of Newcastle on his shoulders and maybe that needed to be taken away from him a little and spread around a bit. Every day, everybody would ask what he was going to do next. Everybody in the club was waiting to see what his next move would be and he needed huge shoulders to carry such a load. He used to say to me, "We've created a monster here, and we've got to keep feeding it!" Maybe he needed a little bit of help to feed it.'

Keegan was undoubtedly less eager to communicate with the media, a part of the job in which he had previously revelled. At the start of the 1996–97 season, it was announced he would talk to the press only immediately before and immediately after a game. Not only that, but all interviews with players had to be arranged through the newly appointed press officer, the former Metro Radio journalist Graham Courtney. In a way, these developments were simply a natural consequence of Newcastle's growth as a club, but the press could not help comparing them unfavourably with the recent past, when it had been virtually open house at St James' Park and Keegan was never too busy to talk to a journalist.

'I've never seen such a change in a man you are dealing with daily,' says John Gibson. 'When he first came to Newcastle as a player, part of the deal was with Newcastle Breweries, who were going to sponsor him – double his wages – and in return he was going to do shows at the local clubs round here. I compèred those shows, worked on stage with him once a week round the Newcastle area, and his enthusiasm then was so infectious, the places were packed out. He'd stay two hours afterwards signing autographs, too.

'He brought that infectiousness into management, not only with the players, but also with the press, the fans, with everybody. He was unquestionably, in all the years I've been in football, the

THE APOCALYPSE

greatest PR that I have ever met – a natural. But in his last few months at Newcastle as a manager, it was almost like seeing a different man both physically – grey hair, strained face – and in terms of someone who was willing to talk not only to the press but to so many people. The pressure and the disappointment got to him and it came as no surprise when he quit. The timing of it was always going to be a surprise, but it was a case of when he was going to finish rather than if.'

Sir John Hall thinks Mark Lawrenson's phrase about the loss of the twelve-point lead knocking the stuffing out of Keegan is particularly apposite. 'That's probably a good simile,' he says. 'When we were so many points ahead, we all expected to win the League. And when it went from us, it took me a month to get over it. So how long must it have taken Kevin? An awful long time, I should think; and he was bound to wonder then whether all the pressure was worthwhile.

'Basically, you've got to ask yourself whether you can sustain it every season. No one outside of football can understand the pressure they put on the people out in front. If the heat gets too hot, then I suppose that's what we are here for; but it's unfair and unjustifiable. If this were any normal business, the press and the fans wouldn't have the right to make the demands on us that they do, but it's a business with so much emotion attached to it – and the pressures upon you due to that emotion are frightening, really. You are playing with people's lives, because people live their lives through the football club and through the players, and we are responsible for that. The trouble is that sometimes you tend to forget it.'

Nevertheless, Hall insists that the Newcastle board made every effort to keep Keegan on the two or three occasions he indicated his desire to leave. Gradually, however, they came to realize that there was a degree of inevitability about the situation. 'I had a lot of time for Kevin,' says the Newcastle chairman, 'and I did not want him to go. All of us thought so highly of him that we said, "Now come on, we'll work this through together." Towards the end, I had him in and said, "Now look, there are times when I've had to fight my way through life and you've got to battle." Then the next day, we went and beat Tottenham 7–1 and he was upset by what that did to Gerry Francis. Only he will know when the decision to go was taken, but I think he had already made up his mind by the time we played Spurs. However long he might have stayed on, I think it had come to the point where he would have wanted to go in the end.'

Above all, Sir John strongly contests any suggestion that Keegan was forced out by the flotation or placed under any unreasonable pressure to raise money by selling players. 'The flotation may have been a part of his going, but only a minor part,' he says. 'When Kevin was unsettled, we could see eventually that his mind was made up to go; and I think they [Keegan, Douglas Hall and Freddie Fletcher] talked about him going on until the end of the season. I wasn't part of the float: I was looking at the football club. And I felt that if he was going to go at the end of the season and his heart wasn't in it, then it might be better from a football point of view if we could replace him quickly.

'We still had a chance of winning the Premiership – it hadn't gone from us. The 1996–97 season was a strange one because no team played consistently well and the title could have been won by anybody who slung a few results together. So, as reluctant as I was to see Kevin go, when I sat down and thought about it I decided that if his heart's not in it any more and there's still a chance of winning the League, why prolong the agony he's in? I told Douglas that I thought we should bring another manager in right away – in any case, Kevin himself kept saying we had to find another manager.'

Hall has a revealing response, too, to Keegan's claim that he had to raise £6 million by selling players to get the bank off the club's back before the flotation. It seems this had everything to do with the record-breaking purchase of Alan Shearer for £15 million. 'To be fair on ourselves,' says Sir John, 'when we bought Shearer, the club really put itself out to pay that kind of fee. We thought we had him for £10–12 million, but then had to go to £15 million with the bank's help. It was a lot of money and we said we'd give it to Kevin provided he reduced the figure by selling players. They all agreed the deal and Kevin was part of it. We had launched ourselves into a £15 million transfer – the top price – and there was an understanding between everybody that we'd gone over budget and would have to reduce that kind of financial outlay. It was the only time we ever stipulated that players had to be sold.'

Whatever the pros and cons of the situation for Newcastle United there was no going back now – the die was cast. Caught between Keegan's determination to go on no further than the end of the season and the technical demands of a flotation on the Stock Market, the club appeared to have little alternative but to pay off, there and then, a man who was certainly the most charismatic manager in their history and arguably the most successful. 'When we were going to float,' points out Sir John Hall, 'we would have had to disclose in the documents that our manager was leaving at the end of the season. And can you imagine the depression that would have caused for the fans and everybody? So it was the inevitability of Kevin's going that determined the timing of it.'

He also points out, with plenty of justification, that Keegan is hardly in a position to complain about having to sell a few players. 'I don't think any manager has been supported the way he was supported,' he says. 'He left a bitter man, but he always had a good deal from us. He probably felt he should have had some shares. Had he stayed, Douglas would have looked after him, but it was his decision to go. It didn't just happen once; and I think when he finally decided to leave, we just felt it was better to let him go.'

And so, sadly, one of the most glorious chapters in Newcastle's history ended in disenchantment as well as disappointment.

9

THE EPILOGUE

Kevin Keegan's resignation as manager of Newcastle United in the early days of January 1997 was certainly the end of the Keegan era at St James' Park; but it was not the end of the story, by any means. Six days later, Keegan was replaced by Kenny Dalglish, the man who had succeeded him as a player at Liverpool twenty years earlier, after Keegan had left to join Hamburg. 'Spooky' is probably the only way to describe such a remarkable coincidence. Thus, the Liverpool connection – and influence – was maintained at St James' Park as Newcastle sought to limit the damaging effects of Keegan's departure by appointing an equally famous manager as quickly as possible.

Bobby Robson had been their first choice, but the former England manager could not be lured away from Barcelona – even though the move would have meant a sentimental return to his native North East. 'I thought the only feller for the job was Bobby Robson,' admits Sir John Hall, 'but he wouldn't come. An honourable man, he said he had a contract with Barcelona he wouldn't break. I was disappointed because I have a lot of time for him and I thought he would have been right for the club in that period as a North Easterner coming home.'

As a result, English football experienced what was possibly its first managerial appointment by television. 'We didn't think we could have Kenny [Dalglish],' explains Sir John, 'because he wasn't in the game any longer, didn't want to come back into football and didn't want to know, so far as we were aware. And these were the only people of the right sort we could consider. Then Alan Hansen said on BBC television that the Newcastle job was tailor-made for Kenny, even though he wasn't in the market place.' Knowing Hansen and Dalglish were close friends, Newcastle correctly interpreted Hansen's casual remark as a signal from Dalglish that he wanted the job. And that was all the encouragement they needed.

Few applicants for the job could have presented more impressive credentials than the forty-five-year-old Scot. A support striker of sublime skill with Celtic, Liverpool and Scotland, Dalglish had done what so few truly talented players do and gone on to be a successful manager. He had collected the coveted League and FA Cup double in his first season as Liverpool's player-manager, 1985–86. Then he won the former First Division title twice more and the FA Cup once more before shaking Anfield to its foundations in 1991 by walking away from the stress of a high-profile job made unbearable for him by the loss of life at the Heysel Stadium in 1985 and at Hillsborough in 1989.

Eight months later, he had recovered sufficiently from that emotional crisis to take the manager's job at Blackburn, where Jack Walker's millions had awoken the former steel magnate's sleepy home-town club with a jolt. And a good job Dalglish did there, too. Promotion to the Premier League in 1992 was followed by the signing of Alan Shearer from Southampton (£3.3 million) and Chris Sutton from Norwich (£5 million). Between them, Sutton and Shearer – known popularly as the SAS – scored most of the goals which carried Blackburn to the Premiership title in 1995, the club's first championship for eighty-one years.

The rest, as they say, is a mystery. After winning the title, Dalglish had moved upstairs as director of football – a job without real meaning – while his former assistant manager, Ray Harford, took over as manager. Dalglish explains in his autobiography that he didn't want any more of the daily grind; yet only a month after leaving Blackburn by mutual consent in December 1996 he agreed to become manager of Newcastle United and take on one of the most onerous and

THE EPILOGUE

stressful jobs in English football ... By then, it was also the best-paid. According to the tabloids, who are never too far wrong in such matters, Dalglish signed a three-and-a-half-year contract worth £1 million a year. It made sense, if only because the ten-year contract Keegan signed in 1994 was said to have been worth £10 million.

Even if Dalglish's salary had been only half that staggering figure, Newcastle's ability to pay it was a striking measure of how far they had come in the five years since Keegan walked out in a huff because the £500,000 promised by Sir John Hall for buying players had not materialized and the Third Division was yawning beneath them. This, too, before the money-raising flotation, the proposed details of which had been released the previous Thursday – the day after Keegan had left. There was no mistaking, then, the conjunction between the three events. Dalglish was brought in quickly to reassure the City as well as to mollify the Toon Army.

But was he capable this time of filling Keegan's golden shoes? Was anyone? Throughout his five momentous years as manager of Newcastle United, Keegan had drawn strength from the almost mystical relationship he had with the club's fans. And that relationship existed only because he had revived the club as a player and had established an open dialogue with the supporters when he became manager. Not only had Dalglish never played for Newcastle, but he also had a reputation for being remote and austere. On the surface, the two men could not have been more different as people. All they seemed to have in common was a love of golf and a lack of coaching qualifications.

While Keegan was extrovert, emotional and dynamic, Dalglish was introverted, taciturn and intense. At least, that was the public perception of them. Those who know Dalglish well talk enthusiastically about his sense of humour and the lighter side of his personality; but all that is displayed in public is a prickly dourness that makes the average television interviewer sweat at the thought of putting a microphone under Dalglish's nose. So, was this the sort of man capable of establishing some kind of rapport with the fans who had idolized Keegan and energized his management of Newcastle United? Only time would tell.

Dalglish certainly made all the right moves and noises as he took over. Asked if he thought Keegan had left Newcastle in the lurch, he snapped, 'I think you're out of order saying that. It's a good lurch to leave them in, isn't it? I don't think there would be too many fans criticizing Kevin Keegan if you look at the work he has done at this club and I go along with that.' He also plugged into the Keegan legend by keeping Terry McDermott, whom he knew well from their playing days at Liverpool, as his assistant manager. 'He's someone I know I can trust,' he said, reiterating the reason Keegan recruited McDermott in the first place.

On the pitch, things didn't begin too well. Newcastle won Dalglish's first match in charge, the replay of their FA Cup third-round tie against Charlton, but were knocked out in the next round at home by Nottingham Forest. In the Premiership there was a 2–2 draw at Southampton followed by three successive wins against Everton, Leicester and Middlesbrough. The 4–3 victory over Leicester at St James' certainly revived memories of the Keegan era with Alan Shearer rescuing Newcastle from a 1–3 deficit with three goals in the last thirteen minutes.

However, after losing to Liverpool 4–3 at Anfield for the second season running and again echoing what had gone before, Newcastle finished the season with a ten-match unbeaten run. It was just powerful enough for them to snatch second place from under the noses of Arsenal and Liverpool, who had been vying with each other for the runners-up spot behind Manchester United. Newcastle rounded off the season with a Keeganesque flourish, too, beating Nottingham Forest 5–0 at St James' Park. It was a turning point in Dalglish's relationship with the fans, according to Steve Wraith.

'That last game was the first time the fans actually chanted Dalglish's name,' Wraith points out. 'It's been hard because the fans have had their songs for five years now and there's that many which revolve around Kevin – the "Keegan Wonderland song", for instance – that people just didn't know what to sing.

THE EPILOGUE

But that last day of the 1996–97 season, when we knew we'd finished in second place, Dalglish's name was reverberating round the stadium. It was fantastic. I think that was the day Dalglish realized he'd finally arrived at Newcastle United.'

It was a major achievement in anyone's language. Considering the traumas the club had had to overcome – a change of manager halfway through the season, followed by a stock market flotation – Newcastle had performed wonders to finish ahead of everyone but Manchester United. As Sir John exclaimed to me in Zagreb at the start of the 1997–98 season, 'It's a miracle!' We were in the Croatian capital because the new bonus for finishing second had been the chance to qualify for a dip into the great honeypot of the Champions League. Thanks to the controversial expansion of the European Cup to include the runners-up, as well as the champions, from Europe's stronger leagues, Newcastle played off against Croatia Zagreb over two legs for the right to go in with the big boys and won. Now they were in a position to earn between £7 and £12 million from a league system specifically designed to generate fortunes for the competing clubs.

So, Dalglish had justified immediately the decision to appoint him and had provided money not only to cover his salary, but for strengthening the squad. That surprised no one less than Ray Harford, the former assistant manager at Blackburn, who had taken over from Dalglish when the enigmatic Scot became director of football. 'It's a certainty that Kenny will win something for Newcastle,' Harford told me shortly after his old boss had been installed at St James' Park, 'and I think he'll do it this year. He'll possibly win the League and probably win the UEFA Cup.' Harford's confidence was not entirely justified, in that Newcastle were promptly knocked out of the UEFA Cup by Monaco and finished only second in the Premiership. Nevertheless, as we have seen, in economic terms that was almost as good as winning the League.

The quarter-final defeat by Monaco (4–0 on aggregate) renewed the doubts about Dalglish's capacity to cope with the demands of European football that had developed while he was with Blackburn. On the night Keegan's Newcastle slaughtered Antwerp 5–0 away in the first round of the 1994–95 UEFA Cup, for instance, Dalglish's Blackburn had lost 1–0 at home to the Swedish part-timers Trelleborgs. They drew the away leg 2–2, but the damage had been done. Because Liverpool had been banned from Europe while Dalglish was in charge at Anfield, that had been his first stab at the European competitions as a manager – and it had ended in ignominy.

So to have overcome a side as talented as Croatia Zagreb, champions of one of the most powerful nations to have emerged from the political fragmentation of the old eastern bloc, must have given him immense personal satisfaction. He did it, moreover, without Alan Shearer, who had suffered a truly horrendous ankle injury in a pre-season match at Everton just before the start of the 1997–98 season, and Les Ferdinand, who was sold to Tottenham for £6 million at just about the same time. (Coincidentally, both had been absent when Newcastle went out to Monaco the previous season.) So there were clear signs that Dalglish was coming to terms with both European football and the manipulation of reduced resources.

He replaced Shearer and Ferdinand with Faustino Asprilla and Danish newcomer Jon Dahl Tomasson, one of his summer signings. Two others, the Italian Under-21 international Alessandro Pistone, and the veteran England international Stuart Pearce, stiffened that suspect defence noticeably, while yet another, balding Georgian international midfielder Temur Ketsbaia, scored the winning goal against Croatia Zagreb in the last minute of extra time. A new goalkeeper was recruited, too, in an attempt to cure the chronic inconsistency there had been in that key position. He was Shay Given, the young Republic of Ireland international, who had grown tired of playing second fiddle to Tim Flowers at Blackburn.

Essentially, however, Dalglish had steered Newcastle into second place in the Premiership with the players he inherited from Keegan. Perhaps the most important change he made was to his midfield. 'It will be interesting to see what he does in the

THE EPILOGUE

short term about sorting out his defence,' Ray Harford had said. 'I think he'll probably fatten up the midfield.'

And that's exactly what Dalglish did do. The most notable casualty was David Ginola, the flamboyant French winger who could be thrillingly effective going forward but who tended to go missing when the opposition had the ball. That unfortunate habit was the reason for the spectacular row that broke out between Keegan and left back John Beresford during a match against Aston Villa. 'Beresford was one of those who felt they carried the can for the style of play demanded by Keegan,' contends John Gibson.

'Kevin, of course, just wanted Ginola to go out and play; but when he didn't have the ball, behind him Beresford would find two opponents coming at him because there's no way Ginola would come back to help. That's what produced the outburst at Villa. Kevin took John to one side afterwards, when everything was patched up in the summer, and said, "I know what your worry is, and you're right: I know you get exposed, but all I can say to you is Ginola can do so much on the ball, I want him in the side. I will stick by you and continue to play you if you will tolerate the fact that you are going to get in a mess from time to time." That was the compromise they reached, although John wasn't too happy because it still meant that, to a certain extent, he was going to look foolish.'

Unsurprisingly, someone as pragmatic as Dalglish was not prepared to tolerate such a potentially self-destructive situation. Ginola, who was out injured at the time the Scot took over as manager, played only three times in the second half of the season and was sold to Tottenham for £2 million the following summer. During that telling run-in over the final quarter of the season, Ginola was supplanted on the left of midfield by Robbie Elliott, the local youngster who had been alternating with Beresford at left back. Elliott is skilful enough to attack, right enough, but he is also conscious of his defensive duties. Nevertheless, he was also sold in the summer and his wing back's job handed over to that great survivor John Beresford as Dalglish set about reshaping the side with a will.

However, for the time being, the new manager had, in Ray Harford's words, 'fattened up' his midfield. He fattened it even further by the occasional use of Warren Barton, that expensive and under-used full back, as a midfield marker. Sadly, one of the casualties of all these changes was Peter Beardsley. Although he could never be accused of neglecting his defensive responsibilities, Beardsley was discarded as readily as Ginola by Dalglish. The player who had done so much to help revive Newcastle playing alongside and under Keegan made only three further League appearances that season. Then, having initially blocked Beardsley's projected transfer to Bolton because of the crisis brought on by the injury to Shearer and the sale of Ferdinand, Dalglish eventually allowed the move to go through.

It was the second time Dalglish had sold Beardsley and the little Geordie imp was, quite obviously, decidedly unhappy about having to leave his home-town club at such a late stage in his career. Dalglish insists that all the speculation about there being bad blood between the two of them and their wives is completely unfounded; but it is otherwise very difficult to understand why the Scot should twice, at Liverpool and at Newcastle, have thought it necessary to dispense with the services of such a talented player – a player very similar in style and ability to himself, in fact. No doubt Beardsley's age – he was thirty-six just after Dalglish's arrival at St James' Park – had once more something to do with it.

Rather surprisingly, Dalglish preferred to put his faith in a maverick, the extravagantly gifted and totally unpredictable Faustino Asprilla. Everyone expected that Asprilla, like Ginola, would be one of the first out the door when Keegan's romanticism was replaced by Dalglish's pragmatism, but everyone was wrong. Dalglish clearly believed Asprilla had more to offer than the simple ability to entertain and backed his judgement by giving the spidery Colombian international an extended run in the side during the second half of the 1996–97 season. Subsequently,

THE EPILOGUE

early the following season, Asprilla responded magnificently to the responsibility of leading the attack – usually on his own – in the indefinite absence of Shearer. He was hugely influential in Newcastle's defeat of Croatia Zagreb, for instance.

Steve Wraith always makes a point of saying he does not speak for Newcastle fans as a whole, but there can be little doubt that most of them would endorse what the editor of the *No. 9* said during the interval between the two seasons in which Asprilla blossomed. 'Those five years under Kevin were fantastic and I don't think we'll ever see a better Newcastle United team, but I think Kenny Dalglish has got the chance to take it on to a higher level. That's what he's here to do. He's won the League as a manager, won it as a player, won caps for Scotland. The bloke's won everything in football, and that can only be good for Newcastle United.

Indeed, Wraith sees no reason why Keegan's departure and Dalglish's arrival should mean that Newcastle will stop playing attractively. 'Blackburn won the title [when Dalglish was manager] with some exciting football,' he reminds us. 'I seem to remember them beating Nottingham Forest 7–0 the season they were defending the title, too. So where does the idea of Kenny Dalglish's teams playing dull football come from? I don't know. It's probably because Blackburn used to go and scrape maybe a 2–1 win at Old Trafford – and do it on a regular basis. That's maybe why people term it dull football, but I don't agree with that at all. Obviously I'd like to see Newcastle win something with dazzling football, but it just doesn't work like that. An entire season's made up of good games, poor games and average games. You are not going to win anything with a season of swashbuckling.

'Next season, it's Dalglish's team and the responsibility for their results is fully on his shoulders. Only then can we start judging Kenny. He deserves the accolades and the praise for finishing in second place, but that was still partly Kevin's team he did it with. I think a lot of the players played for Kevin towards the end of that season [1996–97]. Some obviously had disagreements with him, but that's football. Kevin Keegan did a fantastic job at Newcastle and no one will ever forget him for that, but it's past and gone. He's in the same record books as Jackie Milburn and Hughie Gallacher. He's history now.'

Sir John Hall says something similar with only slightly more restraint. 'The Keegan years, when I look back, were wonderful years. They were wonderful not just for Newcastle United but for soccer. We led the way in a style of play which was refreshing and perhaps ahead of its time. But always in life you've got to learn from the past. We didn't win anything: we were very close there, but you've got to ask yourself, "How do you win?" It's that magic formula which nobody really knows the ingredients of, but you've got to try and analyse it and get it. We hope that, with Kenny here, that will happen now. Nevertheless, we'll look back on the Keegan years with pride. I, certainly, was proud to be part of them.'

What irritated Sir John after the flotation was the spate of stories in the papers suggesting there was friction between himself and Dalglish because the constraints of being a public company had severely reduced the amount of money available for buying players. Hall said he and Dalglish had laughed at the stories over a cup of coffee. Dalglish, for his part, was careful to emphasize that there was no problem at all between him and the Newcastle board. Even so, the suspicion remained that Newcastle, by following several other Premiership clubs in going public, had agreed to have their hands tied by the 'money men' of the City. The feeling in some quarters is that the price such clubs pay for the capital injected by a float is the loss of their freedom to buy and sell players as they want: all their business dealings become shaped by the needs of the Plc.

'There comes a point as a business grows,' argues Hall in reply, 'where you have to manage it in a different way. As the company gets bigger and bigger you introduce good management systems and they, by their very nature, change the entrepreneurial ways you used in the past. What it amounts to is that we have to learn to live with the City and the City has to learn to live

THE EPILOGUE

with football. I think your hands are tied in some ways, but you can't go on continually pumping money into the club as we've done in the past. There comes a time when you have to balance the books – and that goes for any business or any club. We as a family had to ask ourselves whether we wanted to put another £10 million of our own into this, another £50 million of our own into that. You are never given any credit for it, either. It's just a question of, "Oh, well, the bugger's got the money to do it!"

'I'm a strategist, and I said to Douglas, "If you want to consolidate Newcastle, then you've got to look to the future. You've got to take Newcastle into the twenty-first century. It's going to take a lot of money, but I don't think you should risk it now as a family. We've gone through the worst, but there's still a lot to spend. You've got new stadiums to build. We've gone through two stages already. Mark one was the old stadiums and mark two is the ones we've all built of about 40,000 capacity, but the bigger clubs are going to need ones of 50–60,000. That's going to come. Even if digital television comes in and makes it possible to watch your club's every match from your armchair at home, people are going to want a crowd. You could let them in for nothing to provide an atmosphere.

'As things are at the moment, we've got huge waiting lists for season tickets. So unless we build a new stadium or do something to alleviate the situation, we're going to kill off the next generation of fans. It's something that we've really got to look at carefully if we want to fulfil our mission of becoming constantly one of the top three clubs in the UK and one of the top ten in Europe. That means you are competing with the real giants, who've got unlimited funding coming in, whereas we're just a provincial side. We've got a big catchment area and big potential, but we need access to large sums of money. So you either find another rich investor, like Joe Lewis at Glasgow Rangers, or you go to the City. I think more and more clubs are going to be looking for financial partners if they want to stay at the top. The money that will be required for soccer in the future is beyond what any one person or family should commit to the sport.

'At any rate, after talking to a lot of people and getting a report from the bank, it was felt that flotation was the best thing to do. I said it would spread the risk. It paid off debts and consolidated the club, and we now have a platform for the long term. It's up to us to run it as a business, and that's what we are doing. We always have done, but we are doing it now with the discipline of the City as well. And when you are running a multi-million-pound business, that's what you need.'

Contrary to popular belief, the £50 million raised by floating Newcastle United on the stock market was not intended to recompense the Halls directly for their large and life-saving investment in the club. They may have acquired valuable shareholdings as a result of going public, but they had already made sure they were not out of pocket through pouring money into the club. 'We got our money back before the float came,' reveals Sir John. 'The club was doing well, so we gradually got it back. I think our investment reached a peak, in money, guarantees and all the rest, of £12–14 million. Had it all gone wrong, we would have been in for that amount. It was an act of faith, but we had control of it. The float was done for other reasons, as I have explained.'

Some remained to be convinced, however, that Sir John's strategy would work. Shortly before Newcastle played Barcelona in one of the opening matches of the Champions League early in the 1997–98 season, a City expert cast doubt in the *Guardian* on the financial viability of the club's plans. 'I still have the same problem as before: I can't make the numbers out,' Tony Fraher, chief executive of Singer & Friedlander Investment Funds, was quoted as saying. 'The youth policy is not going to kick in for a minimum of six years. Where do they find the money to both replenish the team and build a new stadium?

'They say they are going to do all the work out of retained profits. To do that, they will have to make profits higher than Manchester United. In their original prospectus they said they

THE EPILOGUE

wouldn't be coming back to the City for funding. There's talk of a new bond to finance the new stadium, but I still look at it with some scepticism.'

Fraher also said he found it 'interesting' that Dalglish had sold three local lads, Lee Clark, Robbie Elliott and Peter Beardsley, and signed so many players on free transfers: the implication being that Newcastle's new manager had recruited veterans like Stuart Pearce, Ian Rush and John Barnes not just for their experience but also because it helped balance the books at a time when the club was having to adjust to its new financial constraints. It is certainly interesting to work out the difference between the cost of Dalglish's buying and his selling. At the time of writing, he was something like £7 million in *profit* after signing eleven players and selling only six. Which would suggest that a totally new policy was in effect.

Therefore Newcastle United's move from the Keegan era into the Dalglish era could hardly be called seamless. The team was beginning to undergo major surgery, despite the fact that a much more rigorous attitude to the spending of money had been necessitated by the flotation. The old free-and-easy days of lashing out £60 million on players were over. This meant, of course, that the decisions Dalglish took to buy and sell were of crucial importance, especially in view of the club's continuing ambitions at home and abroad. There was a greater sense of discipline on the field, too, where Keegan's 'fantasy' football had been replaced by Dalglish's more realistic approach to winning. All that remained the same, in fact, was that Newcastle United had still to end their long wait to win something of significance.

10

JOHN AND KEVIN

There are few things sadder than seeing good friends fall out, so one might have hoped for a happier and more suitable ending to the epic, rhapsodical Keegan era at Newcastle United than petty squabbling among the protagonists. Unfortunately, that's how it did end. Seemingly, Keegan was at loggerheads with even his closest allies on the board, Douglas Hall and the two Freddies, by the time he walked away from the job in January 1997, because they were unwilling to go along with his wish to continue as manager only until the end of the season. No doubt further fuel has since been added to the fire, given that Keegan's autobiography was due to be published before this book and the Newcastle directors were expecting anything but praise in it.

It is to be hoped that the former Newcastle manager does at least acknowledge that the long-awaited revivification of the club between 1992 and 1997 was more than a one-man job. It was not just a two-man job, either: the black and white giant was so fast asleep, it needed more than Kevin Keegan and Sir John Hall to shake him awake. All those who helped Sir John and his son to win the long and bitter battle for control of the club must be congratulated. One of them was Freddie Fletcher, the present chief executive, and it must be said that Keegan would not have been appointed had the shrewd little Scot not had the bright, though decidedly risky, idea of bringing him in from eight years in the football cold.

Essentially, this tale is representative of how Keegan's gift for galvanizing and inspiring people, backed by the unswerving support – both financial and moral – of the Newcastle board, rescued the club from relegation to the darkest depths of the Football League and turned them into one of the country's leading lights. Public perceptions being what they are, however, it was Keegan and Hall who were seen as the dream ticket that would transport Newcastle United to the promised land. Not that one half of the ticket saw it quite that way. 'We just got on with the job,' says Sir John. 'When you step back and analyse it, there may be reason to see it in those terms; but, basically, we just got on with the job.'

We are talking about two very strong characters here, two major egos, so it is not difficult to believe the rumours of friction between them. Hall, however, insists there was no problem at all in his relationship with Keegan. 'You get your differences in any walk of life,' he says, 'and we may have disagreed from time to time but, to the best of my knowledge, we never had the sort of row in which I would say, "Why are you doing that?" I like Kevin. I used to go to his house for meals and we went out for meals together. Kevin and his wife, Jean, lived just across the road from us. My wife got on well with them, and I went to see them regularly.' Others have a different tale to tell.

'The fans, who only saw the public face of Kevin, thought he was a little, cuddly, lovely teddy bear,' says John Gibson. 'But like anybody who's successful, he was very ruthless and very unforgiving. Everybody at Newcastle United trod on eggshells, including the people above him – the board of directors. Two of them, Douglas Hall and Freddie Shepherd, dined with him daily. That was their job. They had a tremendous rapport with him and worked very closely with him. But they knew they were dealing with a very strong character.

'I think they handled him very well – a lot of boards of directors wouldn't have been able to handle Kevin. Equally, I don't think Kevin would have worked for a lot of boards of directors. But I do believe John was taken out of the firing line because he was a strong character, like Kevin, and there could have been problems there. John and Kevin, the two great beasts, would have been locking horns all the time if they had had to deal with each other on a daily basis. Having said that, John was very, very supportive of Kevin in terms of not vetoing anything. He was also very aware of the success Kevin was bringing to the club, and if you've got to put the rise and rise of Newcastle United down to any two people, it's got to be John Hall and Kevin Keegan.'

Something which should be evident by now is that Sir John has enduring admiration for the manager who turned Newcastle into a major force once more. He recalls with obvious relish and affection the way the two of them piloted the club into a steep climb from 1992 onwards. 'We did it by the seat of our pants, at times,' he confesses. 'We were newcomers, the both of us, and we drove it through as we would drive a business. I did the business side and he did the football side. I never interfered one iota. How could I possibly tell him what to do? People laugh at me because I still talk about teams in terms of two full backs, three half backs and five forwards! So I stayed out of it. I used to have to say, "At least tell me he's no good!" I knew nothing about footballers and never pretended that I did. I was the businessman behind the club.

'What we did then was get the fans on our side. We used to go round the pubs with the brewery meeting the fans and explaining what we were doing. There would be 400–500 of them in the pub and they appreciated it. We built up a rapport with the fans and we built up a rapport with the press. We were always available, because that's what you've got to do. You know you need each other and sometimes I think we forget that. There's also got to be responsibility from both sides. I think we had it then, and it was a great time. Then we built up and got promotion. That was an unbelievable time: it was so exciting.'

There is no doubt that the principal defining quality of the Hall–Keegan era was the adventurous nature of the football Newcastle played – but spending an unprecedented amount of money on players came a close second. Sir John defends that largesse, however, by arguing that Newcastle had fallen so far behind the leading clubs in English football during their many fallow years that the only way to catch up was to throw cash by the million at the problem.

'When we got into the Premier League,' he says, 'I thought it would take us three years to build a squad that might win something. But the second year was a bonus in that we nearly won the League. We had spent over £50 million on players, but we had built the equity. We gambled a lot, and you had to do that in those circumstances. It was a lot of money to invest, but you had to do that quickly because when I came into football it was changing. European leagues were on the horizon, and if you were not in the top echelon when they were formed, you'd never be there. Newcastle hadn't won anything for years, so we had to make this hard push in order to get there. That was the strategy, the thinking behind it and it worked to a large degree.'

Hall also makes the point that it could not have worked unless the two halves of the partnership had fitted together as if made for each other. 'We gave Kevin the financial backing, and he gave us a platform for the next ten years,' says the Newcastle chairman. 'He couldn't have done it without our money and we couldn't have done it without him. So it was the perfect combination. But I always told him that we needed continuity; we were pushing for things overnight, but we couldn't do things that quickly. I reckoned it would take us three to five years to win something, as it did Alex Ferguson at Manchester United. There's no such thing as instant success unless you are in the drug business, or whatever.'

Like Sir John, Chris McMenemy believes Keegan's great achievement was to have given Newcastle United a platform for the future. The most charismatic manager in the club's history may not have won anything, but he laid the foundations for success. 'I think it did hurt Kevin a bit not to have won anything for the supporters,' says the former chief coach, 'but in a way he did win something for them. I think he knows that and they know that. They've now been given a platform to do something about the problem.

'They had never been regarded as a top four team before. They weren't even bracketed with the likes of Tottenham or Chelsea: they were up and down, they were a cup team. The usual routine was, "They are a sleeping giant who should be doing this, that and the other: they've got a divine right to the title." But now we are in a situation where if Newcastle don't win it the fans will be disappointed. And that's entirely down to Kevin. Whoever came in – and it just happened to be Kenny – would have had a platform to work from which he would never have had before.'

As a native Geordie, McMenemy finds it difficult to conceal his sense of wonder and delight at what has happened to his club in such a short space of time. 'To think that only a few years ago they were nearly relegated to the Third Division. Then, all of a sudden, they bought a few players, played good football, got into the Premier League and now there's every chance they'll go on to greater things. It was just amazing the way it all happened.

'Even now outsiders seem to think that Newcastle, with all that flair and exciting football, must have been a happy-go-lucky club in a lot of ways. But the planning behind it, the organization and the way it was executed from the chairman right the way through was exceptional. I don't think it will ever be repeated. If you look at the top four clubs in the country – Manchester United, Arsenal, ourselves and Liverpool – the other three have been winning things for donkey's years. This club hasn't and the more everybody with their second breath wills Newcastle to do it, the more it is a testament to what has been achieved.'

Above all, McMenemy stands in awe of the energy and commitment, the sheer selflessness that Keegan put into the job. There is no question that he regards the former Newcastle manager as the fulcrum of the whole thrilling balancing act. 'From day one, he's come in here and got his personality across,' says McMenemy. 'You couldn't say exactly how he did it, but it was a question of his personality being expressed right through the club. He drove everything. He drove the football side, he drove the commercial side – you name it, he drove it.

'I didn't see him bothered by any problems or any business he couldn't overcome. He just went charging on all the time. Everything revolved around him. He gave himself to everyone. He wasn't content to sign a few autographs out of ten and then say he was sorry and had to go. He'd sign all ten. And if there was a commercial presentation on in the afternoon he wouldn't forgo the morning's work. He'd do that first, then go to the presentation – then he would go and do something in the evening. He was always giving of himself to the rest of the club, but whether they actually realized that I don't know. I think they did towards the end. He was just a dynamo, really.'

Like McMenemy, Derek Fazackerley, his predecessor as chief coach, argues that what Keegan won for the club should be measured in advancement, not silverware. That may sound like simply avoiding the real issue, but it is not an unreasonable way of assessing those five eventful and dramatic years at St James' Park. Asked to define Keegan's strengths as a manager, Fazackerley says, 'His enthusiasm for the job, his desire to see the club do well. He always said he wanted to provide the public up there, which he has a great affection for, with a football team to be proud of. And without actually winning anything, I think he did do that. Everybody was enthralled by the style of football, the way that the team played and the results that the team got.

'It was a bit cavalier at times, which probably stopped us winning the major honours, but you couldn't deny we excited a lot of people and gave them good entertainment and value for money. Kevin certainly put Newcastle back on the map. They were a talking point not only when they were winning games, but also when they were losing games. There was as much discussion about how Newcastle lost games as about how they won games. Obviously, it was something for television to latch on to. The live games on Sky TV that everyone in the country enjoyed – and Newcastle enjoyed being involved

JOHN AND KEVIN

in – gave the club the sort of national spotlight they were looking for.'

McMenemy, in turn, agrees with Fazackerley on the subject of Keegan's relationship with the fans. He identifies it as a key element in Keegan's managerial style. 'The first couple of years I spent there,' he says, 'Kevin was really special because he knew what the club meant to people. He always considered the supporters – it was another of his strengths, I think. He would never just say, "Get out there and play!", he would always add, "You are lucky to be playing in front of these people!" He said that because he'd played in front of them himself and knew how loyal they'd remained despite being starved of success and entertainment for so long.'

The interesting thing about Fazackerley and McMenemy is that these two men whose interests were essentially in the preparation of the team felt it necessary to mention the contribution to the club's revival made by Sir John Hall. Fazackerley and McMenemy's comments might be mistaken for toadying, were it not for the fact that there is overwhelming evidence that they were evaluating the situation objectively and correctly when they suggested Keegan and Hall were interdependent. 'Because of the finance that was made available to Kevin, I think the chairman being at the club at the same time probably had something to do with the success as well,' concedes Fazackerley. 'And the chairman would leave it to him to manage the football club as he wanted to manage it.' McMenemy was less expansive in his remarks on the subject, but the message was roughly the same. 'The chairman has given the club a financial basis they've never had before,' he said. 'So there's less worry about that side of it now.'

Sir John himself says, 'A few managers have said to us that they wish they'd been given the opportunity that Kevin had. There were no restrictions on him whatsoever and, as you know, the family put a lot of cash in.' He is, however, well aware that there was more to it than money. 'He has – what's the word? – personality, which the fans loved,' adds Hall.

'They'd known him for years, they loved him here and he had his dramatic take-off, etc. Coming back was an inspired signing by Douglas and Freddie, as I've said, and it just gave life to the sleeping giant.'

The former Newcastle chairman also makes the point that the fact that he and Keegan were a couple of novices together in terms of football administration was not necessarily a disadvantage: it gave them a certain freedom to try things that had not been done before. 'I was a newcomer to soccer, he was a newcomer to soccer management and we both had to learn together as we went along. We had to stop from time to time and ask ourselves what we were doing. But as neither of us had been part of the system, we could be innovative: we weren't restricted or hidebound by the conventions of football.'

Keegan was certainly different from the average club manager in his willingness to communicate directly and openly with the fans and the media. The sight of up to 2000 people watching Newcastle train at Durham and Keegan's face-to-face dialogue on the steps of St James' Park with an angry mob following the sale of Andy Cole to Manchester United are now part of the legend. Since the playing fields at Durham are owned by the local university and a public right of way runs through them it would have been impossible to stop the fans converging on the training sessions anyway, but that is not the point. Keegan actively encouraged them to come because he knew many of them did not have tickets to attend matches at St James' Park. In other words, it was their only chance of seeing their heroes in the flesh.

So far as the media were concerned, Keegan's availability and gift for the telling phrase were an absolute godsend after the sheer grind of trying to pin down most other managers and prise some interesting information out of them. Just how hard the former Newcastle manager worked to inform and delight the newspaper radio and television reporters, is conveyed vividly by John Gibson's description of a typical day in the life of Kevin Keegan for just about all but the last of his five years at the club. 'I, or one of the other people from the *Chronicle*, used to go down to the training ground every morning at 9.15 to get Kevin coming in. He would speak individually to every newspaperman, give three radio interviews, perhaps do a television interview and then, at lunchtime, have the full national press corps in.'

As we have seen, that situation changed dramatically at the start of Keegan's final season, 1996–97, with the introduction of a press officer to act as buffer between the club and the media and the stipulation that the manager would give press briefings only immediately before and immediately after matches. 'He wouldn't give them with the buoyancy he had done, either,' observes Gibson. 'He became almost a recluse towards the end. I would say all that happened in the final six months, beginning with the run-in to the season where he blew the twelve-point lead.

'It was incredible to see the different sort of man he became. He had been a newspaperman's dream, and he'd turned into someone who didn't even want to speak. From being a huge extrovert, he'd become reclusive – and it showed. Physically, too, he looked so different from the man we'd all known. You saw the strain he was under when he came out with that outburst against Alex Ferguson on television. That was a man at the end of his tether.'

Now, looking back, Sir John believes Keegan probably made a rod for his own back by being so accessible to the media. While the relationship was wonderful for Newcastle United in public relations terms, it imposed enormous stresses – on the manager, in particular. 'Maybe he was too free with the press,' muses Hall. 'He gave his all, and the demands upon his time became almost unbearable. It was wrong for people and the press to expect it. Nobody understands: it affects your family life, and there's no way anybody should be put under those pressures. The pressures at a club like this were always quite severe; and what Kevin created overwhelmed us in many ways.'

Sir John could easily have been talking about himself as well – and probably was. His sudden decision to retire as chairman at the end of 1997 came as no surprise to me because he had indicated clearly in our talks for this book that, at sixty-four, he had had enough of being responsible for a high-profile and increasingly demanding club like Newcastle. A rich man, he yearned to spend his money and the remainder of his life doing what he and his wife wanted to do, untrammelled by the burdens of chairmanship. Not only that, but he went so far as to say he wished he had never become involved with Newcastle United in the first place.

Asked if he had any regrets about taking on an enterprise as enormous as Newcastle United had become, his reply was emphatic. 'Oh yes, yes, yes, I do,' he said. 'I'm still a reluctant chairman in many ways, because it's affected my private life and personal life. Don't forget that I'm sixty-five next year, and I retired from my businesss [Cameron Hall Developments] when I was sixty. My son runs the business now and what I wanted to do was spend more time with my wife. I'd given up so much, and she'd given up so much, for the football. The demands on me were tremendous – opening places, etc. People don't understand what it's like; but if you don't do it, they say you are getting above yourself and I'm very conscious of that because I've never lost touch with my roots.

'Basically, I've enjoyed what I've done, but I still feel cheated in some ways that I haven't been able to do the things that I want to do personally. What my wife and I planned to do when I was sixty has not been achieved. I want to travel, I want to read a lot more, I want to write books. When you've had to build a business up, you've done nothing else but work, and there comes a time when you've got to say enough is enough. There have to be other things in life, there has to be more time for the intellectual side of it. I'm not particularly intellectual, but I've got an enquiring mind. I want to get at the Internet now, I want to have an influence on my grandchildren. I want to take them through life and the Greek civilizations – my son-in-law is Greek. I want to take them for a holiday. Basically, I just want to sit down and not talk business.

'I've enjoyed what I've done, but if I had the choice again

JOHN AND KEVIN

I don't think I would have done it had I known what I was getting into. I'll never really cease to be the reluctant owner of a football club. Of course it's given me great satisfaction to have released the giant here at Newcastle United: we've given people their pride back. But it's been at a cost to my personal life. I've worked since I was eighteen, and now I'm nearly sixty-five. I don't want to see fifty years in work, as my father did down the pit and got nothing for it – there comes a time in life when there have to be other things to give yourself.

'Running Newcastle United is an adrenalin rush, but I've robbed my wife and family of our own private life. We *have* no private life: just look at the press, just look at the dirt they try to dig up now. That's part of the price you pay for being a high-profile figure, I know, but there's sometimes not the sense of responsibility in the media that there should be. I feel sorry for my wife in some ways – I think I've been rather hard on her. She's stuck by me all these years and is a real treasure. We've been married for over forty years, which is a long time. She's had to put up with such a lot and take so much pressure. It's wrong to expect her to go on taking it, and I feel now I've got to spend more time with her. After all, I haven't got that many summers left.'

Inevitably, there were those in the media who refused to believe the straightforward reasons Sir John gave for wanting to retire. They were convinced there must be some ulterior motive, some dark secret from the past, that was responsible for his decision to step down. However, so far as I was able to ascertain, the simple truth is that he had had enough of the pressures. He had not decided to retire when he spoke to me in Newcastle and Zagreb in August 1997, but what made up his mind was a telephone call he received at his second home in Spain during the first week in September. It informed him that his best friend, someone he had known since they were eleven and fellow-pupils at Bedlington Grammar School, had developed a serious, life-threatening illness. It was that shock, that reminder of his own mortality, which prompted him to announce his retirement shortly before Newcastle's opening fixture in the Champions League, a glamorous and testing home game against Barcelona. If you think about it in that context – not to mention the possible effect his retirement could have on the share price – the timing could not have been determined by anything but emotion.

Much was also made in the press of the fact that Keegan's autobiography would not be sold at St James' Park and at the club shops around the town. It was interpreted as a ban imposed by Sir John and his board in anticipation of the criticism of them their former manager's book was expected to contain. In fact, nothing could have been further from the truth. The club's policy always has been to sell only books it has produced or commissioned itself, plus the autobiographies of players currently on the staff. And, clearly, Keegan's *magnum opus* did not come into that category.

11

IN RETROSPECT

Just how good a manager was Kevin Keegan? How will Newcastle and posterity remember him? Any answers to those questions could be embarrassingly premature since as I write his return to football with Fulham has just been announced. However, it is necessary for the purposes of this book to try to evaluate the man's contribution between 1992 and 1997, not only to the revival of Newcastle United but also to the well-being of English football in general. For there is no question that by deliberately building an attacking team and insisting it went forward all the time, Keegan challenged a lot of cherished beliefs and stirred a major debate about how the game should be played.

The season that Keegan's Newcastle gained promotion to the Premier League, 1992–93, the first Premiership title was won by Manchester United. It proved to be the first of many for a team that under the shrewd and inspiring management of Alex Ferguson increasingly got the balance right between defence and attack. The four seasons immediately preceding United's emergence, however, had been dominated to a large extent by the extreme and deadening pragmatism of George Graham's Arsenal. They had won the old First Division title twice in that period and were completing the FA Cup and League Cup double in 1993 just as Newcastle were preparing to join the elite.

Theirs was a record of success that provided ample support for the popular view that the way to win things in English football was to have a cast-iron defence, get the ball forward early and not worry too much about the niceties of the game. It was essentially a counter-attacking strategy that worked better away from home because the opposition were duty bound to attack you there. At Highbury, where they had to take the initiative, Arsenal's lack of a creative midfield often proved a handicap. It was also extremely tedious, as the fans of other clubs were not slow to let the Gunners know. 'Boring, boring Arsenal' became a chant that rang round every Premier League ground in the country. The Arsenal fans eventually turned those taunts against their tormentors with their own ironic response of 'One-nil to the Ars-en-al' sung to the tune of the Pet Shop Boys' 'Go West' and intended to celebrate the fact that, although their team didn't score many goals, they did tend to win.

Kevin Keegan's approach to the game was the antithesis of that philosophy. He wanted to win by as many goals as possible. He didn't mind how many the opposition scored, either, as long as Newcastle scored more. It was a totally new and refreshing attitude that quickly caught the imagination of a public force-fed on pragmatism and growing very tired of it. New is probably not the right word to use, since all Keegan was doing was trying to recreate the past. He almost certainly wanted his team to play with the freedom sides used to in the 1970s, when he was a player and caution was a word worshipped only by Don Revie and Leeds and negatory tactics still hadn't had much of an impact on English football.

There was also, according to some, a calculated desire to be different. 'Kevin's real dream,' maintains John Gibson, 'wasn't just to win the Premier League championship, it was to win it the way nobody had ever won it before. I talked to Darren Peacock and quite a few of the Newcastle players after he went and they said it was the impossible dream, the wonderful dream he had. Even the Liverpool side he'd been in and the other great sides of the period, like Leeds, had never won it the way he wanted to win it. He wasn't content just to win the championship, although that was his goal: he wanted to win it the way no other side had won it. He wanted to win it 4–3 every game, not 1–0.

IN RETROSPECT

'Since he left and they've been able to evaluate what was there, the Newcastle players have said it would have been the greatest achievement in football if, when they were those twelve points ahead, they had won the title because Newcastle were, without a shadow of doubt, the entertainers of the whole country. Kevin, being Kevin, wanted to win it that way. He didn't mind letting in three goals because he believed Newcastle would score four. Now that is a wonderful way to look at football. It's the ideal way of looking at football. But doing that for nine months had never been done. I'm of the opinion that it never will be done and it certainly won't be done under Kenny Dalglish because he won't play it that way.

'But Kevin always wanted to be a one-off in everything he did in life. It wasn't enough for him to win the title in an orthodox way. He wanted to win it in a way and with a side that would stay in the memory – not just of Geordies but of the whole country – for the next fifty years. He said repeatedly, often with some aggression and irritation, "I will walk out of this club before I change the way I play." That was regardless of results, regardless of what the fans might say. He would then insist at length that the fans liked Newcastle to play that way, which was very true. But the whole truth was that Kevin liked Newcastle to play that way: Kevin played that way for his own sake.'

Anyone who thinks Gibson is way off beam here should listen to Derek Fazackerley. The former chief coach does not probe as deeply into Keegan's psyche as the journalist, but he does echo the general tenor of his argument. 'You would never change Kevin and his philosophy,' says Fazackerley. 'It was something that he knew the public wanted and that's what he wanted to give the public. Deep down, he wants to be popular himself. That's in no way being derogatory, or anything like that – it's understandable because of the affection he had for the people and the affection the people had for him.'

Keegan certainly had every right to think it was the right way to play after saving Newcastle from relegation to the Third Division and taking them up into the Premier League. Given that record of achievement, there was good reason for him to believe he had stumbled across a long-forgotten formula for winning things that could take everyone by surprise. He was hardly likely to be persuaded otherwise, either, when Newcastle finished second in the Premiership on their debut and soon established themselves as an equal among the country's leading clubs.

Looking back on that golden period, Fazackerley remembers the good times and thanks his lucky stars he was part of it all. 'Football clubs are great places when things are going right,' he says. 'Nobody asks too many questions; you just go out and play, enjoy yourself, come back in the next day, do a little bit of training, there's a game again on Wednesday, go out, win. It's the greatest thing in the world when it's like that – and it was like that for four years, with only the odd hiccup, really.

Having played at Blackburn for sixteen or seventeen years, or whatever it was, I'd never had the opportunity to play for a big football club. So it was a great education for me and something I'll always look back on with a degree of pride and enjoyment because I was part of what happened. You can be in football for a long, long time and not have the opportunity to work with something like that.'

Persuading Keegan to think again about anything was not the easiest of tasks, in any case. Stubbornness, it seems, was second nature to him. 'It was very difficult to change Kevin's mind,' says John Gibson. 'If only one person has done it, they'll be lucky. The only exception I can think of was when he walked out on Newcastle very early on because he said their promises hadn't been kept and Terry McDermott persuaded him overnight to change his mind. I can't remember him ever changing his mind otherwise.'

Conceivably, there is one other instance. It was when Keegan brought in Mark Lawrenson as a specialist defensive coach the season after Newcastle had frittered away their twelve-point lead – the season in which he resigned. The appointment seemed to suggest that Keegan had finally admitted to himself, in the

IN RETROSPECT

face of growing criticism from the media about Newcastle's defensive frailty, that he would not win anything unless he did something to tighten up his defence. That is certainly how Lawrenson interprets the development.

'Kevin's own words to me when he brought me in were that he'd kind of neglected what had been happening at the back because he was so involved with trying to make Newcastle an unstoppable force going forward. My brief was to come and have a look, talk to players, talk to him and offer my opinions. And that's all I did, really, because he was gone in no time. I came in the October and he was gone in the January. But he knew that if they were going to win the League in his time there, he would have to change the style.

'He didn't want it to be obvious, though: he didn't want to change the fact that people would come from miles around to watch his team play. I think he'd got great pride in that. Even in London, the supporters of other clubs would stop him in the street and say, "I'd pay money to come and watch your team!" He liked that.'

Although Keegan had apparently swallowed his pride and appointed a defensive coach, the rumour-mill insisted it was a change of purely cosmetic value. According to the wagging tongues, Lawrenson might have been allowed to sit on the bench at matches but he was not actually allowed to school the defence in training. 'I didn't have any alternative for a while,' says Lawrenson. 'We had one or two discussions and I started to do things with the defence, but then Kevin was gone.' Lawrenson himself lasted only until the start of the following season, 1997–98, when Dalglish made several changes to his back-room staff. The parting was by mutual consent and Lawrenson returned quite happily to his previous career in television and radio. (As everyone should know by now, he has become one of the team of pundits on BBC TV's Saturday night institution *Match of the Day*.)

Some may have seen Keegan's appointment of Lawrenson as an admission of failure, or even a panic measure – but not

Chris McMenemy. Far from treating it as a sign of weakness in his ex-boss, Newcastle's former chief coach regards the appointment as an example of Keegan's pragmatism and gift for doing something different. 'I think it was probably the turning point, when Kevin brought in Mark,' says McMenemy. 'I think he had possibly realized that to go a little bit further, to get to the next level, we had to tighten up a bit more at the back. It was a great step to bring in a defensive coach, because no one had ever done that before. It was an American football type of thing, where there is an offensive coach and a defensive coach.

'Kevin was very forward-thinking. As chief coach, I had to look at the overall picture, while Terry Mac, as a former midfielder, was more concerned with the midfield. So to get Mark in was quite an interesting step. I think it was probably the right thing – and a clever thing – to do, if only because it appeased quite a lot of the media side of it. He brought in someone who was a great defender, who had a great knowledge of defending and who had a connection with the Liverpoool side that Kevin and Terry played in. It probably wasn't an admission, but an acknowledgement that, to go to the next level, we had to do that certain thing. He'd taken that part of the team so far and we'd reached a certain level, but he wanted to go that bit nearer to winning something.

'The appointment was typical of Kevin because nobody had ever done it before and it was high-profile. Nobody expected it and he did it. Mark probably made a difference in that he could talk to Philippe Albert and Darren Peacock with a great deal of authority because he was a real class defender. His presence may not have done much structurally, but it did affect the defenders mentally: it gave them a little bit of succour when they needed it because they were getting hammered from all parts. Yet they are good defenders – Philippe Albert wouldn't have been to two World Cups with Belgium otherwise and Darren Peacock has turned into a very consistent member of the defence.'

The arguments about that Newcastle defence are likely to

rage for ever more. While most outsiders saw it as the team's Achilles heel, most insiders felt there was nothing wrong with it: the weakness, they believed, was exaggerated by the media. 'I think nowadays it's difficult because of Sky Television,' says McMenemy. 'They've got to pinpoint something, and because we'd scored more goals than nearly every team in the League, for us it was our defence. We'd had a couple of games which finished 4–3 and entertained the nation, but that wasn't enough for people. They had to pick on our defence.

'At the time, I think we'd let in a few more goals than Man. United, three more than Liverpool. We'd all let more in than Arsenal, the perennial good defence. So I think it was just flavour of the month to have a go at the defensive side of it. It didn't bother us because we thought we were a good, well-organized team. It was just that the pressure mounted and snowballed, as it does these days. We all know the rules and what's going to go on; it was just something that stuck at the time.

'I don't think we were ever *not* defensively sound. We organized the team as most coaches and managers would, with the emphasis not just on attack but on defence as well. People have said we never worked on defence in training, but that's just not true. Of course we worked on it. People have said it was a warm-up and five-a-side club, but it wasn't. We worked on functional things, we worked on the basics of play, we worked on all the things football clubs work on. You've got to, otherwise you are not going to do anything at Premier League level.

'We didn't think about changing because we didn't think we needed to. But then, all of a sudden, everyone in England is saying, "You've got to work on this, you've got to work on that." The pressure mounts and you probably do change your outlook. I don't think you consciously say, "Right, this morning we've got to do something different to make us better as a defensive team", but the outside pressures do have an effect.'

While McMenemy's loyalty to Keegan is admirable, he is

almost certainly in a minority in thinking that no change was necessary to improve Newcastle's defensive soundness. In the opinion of most other experts, what was required was a stiffening of the midfield to give the defence more protection. As Mark Lawrenson says, 'I really think they should have won the League in the 1995–96 season. If you are twelve points clear, out of all the other competitions, have only the League to concentrate on and don't have any major injury problems, you must stand a fair chance. And Kevin could have done it if he'd altered the system just very, very slightly. But he didn't want to betray his principles.

'All that was required was for him to err on the side of caution in some games, that's all. Maybe just an extra midfield holding player to release the likes of Beardsley, Ferdinand and Asprilla so that they could get forward and get the goals. When you've got players like them in your team and you've got a defensive platform, you are always going to win more games than you lose. But I think Kevin wanted it free-flowing in all departments and that doesn't necessarily happen. With that slight alteration, they could and should have won the League.'

Derek Fazackerley, however, sees no point in crying over spilt milk here. When I asked him how he thought Keegan's Newcastle had acquired their reputation for being unable to defend a lead, he replied, 'I don't know, really. I was there for the first two years in the Premiership and it's difficult for me to say anything. I have my own ideas – we all have – about the reasons why, but it's never, ever one thing. Quite possibly, we could have been stronger in the middle of the park, which would obviously have taken a little bit of pressure off the back four.

'Invariably, when you are conceding goals it's the back four and the goalkeeper who take the brunt of the criticism, but it's very rarely that one thing. It usually starts further forward than that. But I wouldn't get involved in criticizing the style of play or saying who was to blame for what. I don't think there's any mileage in it, to be honest. Kevin's Newcastle were what they were, they enjoyed doing it, people enjoyed watching it and people should accept it for what it was instead of trying to lay blame.'

Lawrenson is of the opinion that Keegan would have changed, would have modified his attacking instincts, if he had stayed on as manager of Newcastle United. Lawrenson's own appointment, he feels, was indicative of that. He also believes that Keegan would have strengthened his defence with some high-class signings, as Kenny Dalglish has done. 'I think that was the next step for him,' says the former defensive coach. 'Although his existing defenders weren't bad by any stretch of the imagination, I think Kevin realized he had to buy some better players in terms of defensive security. When you consider he'd bought world-class players in people like Shearer, Asprilla, Ferdinand and Ginola, and then look at what he bought defensively ... They were good players, but they weren't on the same kind of plane as the forwards he bought.'

The defenders themselves would argue with that assessment, however. Their contention is that they were made to look worse than they actually were by the ultra-adventurous system Keegan insisted on playing. As John Gibson reports, 'The defenders have said to me since – the defenders who are still at Newcastle – they felt that, individually, Newcastle had a superb defence and if at any stage they'd been sold individually to Manchester United or Liverpool, they would have looked good defenders. But, at Newcastle, they were encouraged to go forward and get horribly exposed.

'Philippe Albert, for instance, was encouraged to go over the halfway line and play on the edge of the other team's box – leaving Darren Peacock vulnerable to a quick counter-attack. The two full backs poured forward at every opportunity, too. That's the way Kevin liked it and that's the way it worked, to a certain extent. But the crowd didn't realize the defenders were being exposed because of the way Kevin was asking the team to play, and the defence carried the can. They were ridiculed regularly and they found it very hard to take.'

Left back John Beresford confirmed that assertion early in the

1997–98 season. Having been converted, with great success, into a goal-scoring wing back by Dalglish, Beresford was talking to the *Sun* with undisguised enthusiasm about the difference the switch to a five-man defence and the introduction of Stuart Pearce's noisy, combative presence had made. 'It has annoyed the lads in previous seasons when people have gone on about the defence,' Beresford was quoted as saying. 'The defence has been fine. It was just the way the set-up was in the Keegan days. He didn't believe in being defence-minded. Winning games was all about scoring more goals than the opposition. In Stuart, we have a natural leader . . . The back four I've played in has been mainly quiet and we needed someone at the back to organize us.'

By banking everything on attack, as well, and not having another string to his bow, Keegan encouraged Newcastle's opponents to take appropriate counter-measures. Managers and coaches in the Premier League monitor other teams and they soon cottoned on to the fact that the Magpies found it difficult to fly backwards. 'In the season Newcastle blew their twelve-point lead,' recalls John Gibson, 'I saw them at St James' Park playing Manchester United, who are one of the greatest counter-attacking sides there are. Newcastle massacred them up to half-time and only Peter Schmeichel's presence kept them in the game. Then Newcastle were taken twice on the counter-punch in the second half – and taken easily because of failure at the back. I think they came up against sides in the Premier League that could counter-punch much better than those they'd met in the First Division.

'Even in games they lost, Newcastle had tremendous pressure, tremendous spirit and entertained more than the other side did, but they got suckered on the counter-punch. Fans of both teams would come away from the game saying, "Newcastle were unlucky. Didn't they play well?" Yes, but they were counter-punched, and good sides do that. You are only supposed to win a game, you are not supposed to dominate it. It doesn't matter how you win it, you win it. Arsenal were a great example of winning things 1–0 and, sadly, that's the way championships are won. Sadly because Keegan did have the right idea about the way the game should be played.'

The voice of the media is supported here by the voice of the experienced ex-professional. Like Gibson, Mark Lawrenson applauds Keegan's attempt to entertain consistently, but doubts whether such idealism could survive prolonged exposure to the gruelling nature of an English football season. 'You've got to get things at the back right before you do anything,' he asserts. 'It's not an ideal world, and you are not going to win 4–3 every week. In the Premier League, you've got to expect to go to certain places and scratch out a result. There are not that many who can play really attractive football and win – ask Manchester United. They have struck the perfect balance between defence and attack.

'If Newcastle had won the title when they were twelve points ahead, it would have been the green light for that open, attacking style of play. They should have won it, too. They had that six months when Ginola was in his pomp and they were irresistible, absolutely irresistible. I think it was the old confidence factor at work: you know, confidence breeds confidence. They just thought they could go anywhere and beat anybody. And for those six months, they did. They did it this season [October 1996], too, when they beat Manchester United 5–0 at St James' Park. You could feel that coming. The problem was, how many of the Manchester United displays were going to win you the League? It wouldn't be enough.

'Realistically, I don't think it's possible to win the major honours playing that way – not in today's football. People talk about teams being so well organized and tactically aware these days, and they are. When you come to the big games where the points really matter, teams just sit back and say, "Go on then. Try and play through us." Another thing about Newcastle in Kevin's reign was that teams always thought they could score against them. It suited Kevin because he knew he had better players going forward than the opposition and were going to score.

'But what happened from around August 1996 until Kevin left in January 1997 was that teams had started to work Newcastle out. They knew what their strengths were; they knew that if you stopped Ginola going round the outside, for instance, he'd come inside and play a bad ball. Teams in the Premier League are not stupid – they work things out. That's why, if you win the title – or something else – the next season is always the major test, because teams do actually go out to stop you playing. And 1996–97 was Newcastle's third season in the Premier League.

'For that reason teams like Manchester United have to be applauded for achieving the sort of consistent success that Liverpool used to have. It's a case of being pragmatic. There are times when you have just got to forget about playing decent football, go somewhere and, within reason, win at whatever cost. I think Kevin would probably regard that as ugly. I think he described going to places like Derby and winning as an ugly victory. But I don't think there's such a thing in the Premier League – there can't be.

'He struck a marvellous blow for attacking football and did so much else besides. All right, he spent millions, but you've still got to go out and buy the right players. There's nothing wrong with striving for perfection, either – especially as he knew that's what the supporters wanted – but I think that's just what he fell down on.

'It's sad. For what Kevin did for Newcastle in those five years, he deserved to win at least one trophy. It doesn't matter what – just one trophy. He was always having to deal with the fact that he did everything for the club and rightly got the praise and the plaudits, but – and it's a big but – he still hadn't won anything.'

Derek Fazackerley begs to differ here. He challenges the view that it is impossible to win anything playing the way Keegan's Newcastle did and argues, a little unconvincingly, perhaps, that Liverpool and Manchester United have proved it. 'Newcastle came very, very close to winning the title last season [1995–96],' he said, 'and I don't think the way they played stopped them winning it. I don't know whether, given the chance again, Kevin might possibly have changed things in one or two matches that they were winning and went on to lose, but Manchester United have managed to harness both. They play attractive football and they defend well when they need to. Then there's Liverpool: there wasn't a more entertaining club in the country than them when they were winning things. Yet they could defend at the same time.

'I think Newcastle had to be applauded for what they tried to do. I think football has changed in the last six or seven years. There is a great desire to entertain and to play the game in what seems the right way. We went through a period in the early eighties, say, where there tended to be a lot of teams playing the long-ball game, or whatever you want to call it. And I think the teams that wanted to change that have shown a great deal of responsibility, if that's the right word. They way they play is more pleasing for the public, although, at the end of the day, if your football team's winning it doesn't really matter which way they play. You are just happy to see them win . . . Except at Newcastle, that is.'

The criticism of Keegan as a manager falls into three main categories: his obsession with attacking football, his suspect temperament and his controversial decision to scrap Newcastle's reserve team. The latter was taken at the start of the 1996–1997 season, Keegan's last, when the Pontins League, in which the reserve teams of the Premier League and Football League clubs compete, refused to extend the dispensation that had allowed Newcastle to play their home reserve matches at the Gateshead Stadium, first because of a newly laid pitch and then because St James' Park was one of the venues for Euro '96.

It was a curious decision – one of Keegan's typically impulsive decisions, reckons John Gibson – that Keegan said he wanted to protect the turf at St James' Park, yet Newcastle would have had to play no more than six reserve team matches at home during the season. As ever with these things, there was more to it than met the eye. Chris McMenemy explains: 'The surface at Gateshead Stadium is very good, but when we were playing there and had a lot of games on it was not one some of the players looked forward to playing on. And the distances we were travelling in midweek also had a bit of bearing on it.

'We didn't have a huge squad, either. People think we had thirty or forty players, when in fact we only had about twenty-two pros you would regard as first-team squad members. There were also two or three pros who were too young to be playing with the seniors, but too old for the kids. So there wasn't really a reserve squad as such. It was made up of some of the better kids and, more often than not, it was predominantly YTS players playing, plus one or two pros that you could probably risk getting injured with a view to the next game on a Saturday.

'Not only that, but the kids were playing a game on a Saturday and also a game in midweek. And I don't think Kevin felt that he wanted to ask some of his first-team players to travel all the way to London on a Saturday to play Arsenal, come back and then travel all the way down to Walsall, Aston Villa or wherever, to play in midweek as well. I think some of his ideas were based on his experience in Germany. When he was at Hamburg, they didn't have a reserve team – I don't think there is a reserve league in Germany. I don't think Spain has one, either. Abroad, generally speaking, you go from the kids team to a nursery side and then into the first team.

'Again, it was a typical Kevin Keegan decision. It was something that hadn't really been done for quite a few years, if ever at this level. People are now saying it hasn't worked and shouldn't have been done, but there are different ways of doing things.'

The main thrust of the criticism was that Keegan had deprived his fringe players of a way of keeping in trim and his up-and-coming youngsters of an opportunity to develop their skills. It was answered by the friendly matches Keegan organized for his second team against opponents like Hearts and the contention that properly structured training sessions were every bit as helpful in the development of players. 'I don't think not having a reserve team hampered the development of any of the players,' insists Chris McMenemy. 'I think people like Darren Huckerby and Chris Holland would gain immeasurably more from training with the first team squad day after day than they would from playing with some of the YTS boys against other YTS boys on a pitch three and a half hours away. That was Kevin's view and that was my view.

'They had the chance to train with international players every day of the week. Chris Holland was in my youth team when they won the league and he sort of graduated up into the reserves and then more or less straight into the first-team squad. When Darren Huckerby came in from Lincoln he was too old for the kids, so he always trained with the first team – and he came on in leaps and bounds just because he was training with very, very good players.

'The only thing they were missing out on was ninety minutes of match practice, which you could get by having practice matches within your own club and which we did have a habit of organizing. Kevin organized several against people like York City and other teams. They sent their first team and we played behind closed doors. That would give the lads the match practice they needed without having to sit on a coach for three and a half hours.

'The people who were present at the time all agreed that it was probably a good thing to do. Jeff Clarke, who was manager of the reserve team, and other people like myself, Terry Mac and a lot of the staff all agreed with the decision [to scrap the reserve team] and thought it was the right one. It was relevant to the squad of players we had and it was relevant to the kids, because they were having to play way too many games. I think a lot of kids do.

'Different clubs will tend to use them to fill out a reserve team, saying they are getting good experience when, really, they are probably better staying at their own age level and learning among their peers. When they come up against a club that happens to put out a lot of pros one week and they get beaten 4–0 or 5–0, people will say it's good experience. But it isn't because they are not playing amongst their own age group.

'Abroad, you would never get away with it. There they are allowed to develop at their own pace and at their own level. Eventually, we tended to play most of our games with a full complement of kids who were also playing on a Saturday at their own age level. And even though they did quite well – got promoted from the second division to the first – we didn't think it was too good for them having to play that much football.

'It was an ongoing thing. Week to week we'd look at the situation and say the squad of players we had at the time was twenty to twenty-five YTS players, two or three who were in between and then a first team squad of eighteen to twenty. The lads who were on the fringe of the first team squad, like Paul Kitson, Chris Holland and Darren Huckerby, were the only ones generally playing in the reserve side. The rest of it was the kids who played at Under-nineteen level. They'd sometimes have Kitson on his own, or Kitson and Holland, having to play in amongst all the kids, which is a bit soul-destroying for the one or two pros who've got to do that. If it was a different squad of players – nine or ten who were together each week – you would say that's the best thing for them to be doing. But it wasn't.'

The trouble is that now Kenny Dalglish has decided Newcastle need a reserve team, they have had to rejoin the Pontins League at the very bottom, in Division Three, where the competition is at its poorest. And for all the theorizing among Keegan's staff about the questionable need for a second team, there is no doubt that it was missed by players out of favour or coming back from injury. 'With not having a reserve team now, it's very hard to keep going,' said John Beresford. 'I was called up out of the blue for the Blackburn game [on 14 September 1996] – I hadn't played for over two weeks and it is hard to settle into a game. Everyone knows how quick the Premiership is and all I'd been doing was training. You need a bridge between training and regular first-team football. Nobody's ever won anything from just the starting line-up.'

Not only that, but Keegan did not really bring through any of the talented young players in which the North East has been traditionally rich. Steve Watson, Lee Clark and Robbie Elliott, the three local youngsters who made it into the first team, were actually signed by Jim Smith. As for Kitson, Holland and Huckerby, they are all with different clubs now and looked as though they couldn't wait to leave Newcastle and get some regular first-team football. Clark and Elliott, too, have moved on, though some of the decisions to sell were down to Dalglish as well as Keegan.

It is only fair to also make the point that the wholesale reconstruction of Newcastle had to be carried out so urgently that it did not allow much scope for the nurturing of the young. It was mainly a question of buying and buying big, a job Keegan did very well on the whole – it would certainly be untrue to say that any of his major signings were a waste of money. They all did a job for him in one way or another and Faustino Asprilla, in particular, proved his value beyond all doubt when the sale of Les Ferdinand and the serious injury suffered by Alan Shearer left the eccentric Colombian as Newcastle's only recognized striker at the start of the 1997–1998 season.

So we come to the issue of Keegan's temperament, the other question mark against his ability as a manager. Ever outspoken, John Gibson says, 'I was convinced he wasn't suited to being a manager, absolutely and totally convinced. He wore his heart on his sleeve, he didn't like pressure and I wouldn't have thought the daily involvement of the job, which is huge in terms of scouting and everything else, appealed to him.

'He's not a man who would take lightly to anything he would see as interference from the board of directors. That would be seen as something horrendous. In reality, it wasn't interference, it was just someone else having a point of view which they wished to express. In fairness to the Newcastle board, I must say that I've never known a Newcastle United manager be given as much leeway as he was – he did virtually run the club – but they felt it was worth it because of what he was giving the club.

'Nevertheless, Kevin is not a natural manager at all – it doesn't suit his nature. Playing did. When he was a player, Kevin Keegan was in charge of himself and that was the end of it. The same applies to any other footballer. When you are managing a club, you lose that sense of self-control. You have got people in charge of you and you are in charge of a large group of people you have to persuade to do your bidding.'

Again, Gibson's view is supported by the opinion of someone who was even closer to the reality of the situation. 'Kevin's highs were so high and his lows so low, he was like a rollercoaster,' says Derek Fazackerley. 'I think he was possibly too emotional to be the manager for a longer period of time. I think you've got to be a little bit more detached, a little bit more on an even keel. Because of his desire to win something for the club, he put himself under enormous amounts of strain and pressure and, in the end, I think that told on him. It certainly made the decision to leave easier for him in some respects.'

This combination of stubbornness, volatility and pugnacity in Keegan's personality also made him someone it was inadvisable to rub up the wrong way. That is not necessarily a bad thing in a football manager, however, especially in these days of sky-high wages and player independence that have made it more difficult than ever to impose discipline upon footballers. In fact, Keegan's tendency to go into black, menacing moods was probably a distinct advantage so far as his job was concerned.

'Here's a man,' says John Gibson, 'who, if he thought he was right and other people were doing things that were wrong, pulled the shutters down; and getting them back up was bloody difficult. I think it would be fair to say that while the players hugely respected him because of his playing record, and hugely liked him in the main because he is a very likeable man at his shining best, there was also a definite "fear factor," which is perhaps a good thing in football – you don't want too soft a manager.

IN RETROSPECT

'A lot of players would say regularly during his reign, "I can't afford to cross the gaffer!" If you did cross him, you were in trouble. John Beresford, who was out of line and admitted he was out of line by getting involved in that heated exchange with Keegan during a match against Aston Villa, told me on several occasions he was absolutely mortified because he thought his feet would never touch the ground again at Newcastle United. He was eternally grateful that, for once, Keegan took no action.'

Derek Fazackerley was certainly conscious of that tougher side of Keegan's nature. 'Although he wasn't a strict disciplinarian, or anything like that,' he says, 'if anyone crossed him, they very soon found their way out of St James' Park. It was just his desire to win things for Newcastle United at work, I think. If he thought they weren't on the same wavelength as him and not pulling in the same direction as him, then nothing would get in his way and they would have to go.'

For the most part, it must be said, it seems that Keegan got on famously with his players. Indeed, the bond he had with them for most of his five years in charge of Newcastle would appear to have been one of the main reasons for the club's success. 'Motivation,' says Mark Lawrenson, 'was one of his main strengths as a manager and that was largely because the players really had respect for him. They liked him as a manager and as a person. They knew that if they had a problem, they could go to Kevin and he would help them. He would always be honest with them and it was very rare for him to criticize them in public. He would always give them the benefit of the doubt, too, because he'd been there: he knew what it was about. His own achievements as a player also helped persuade people like Ginola, Albert and Asprilla to come to Newcastle. It was probably one of the deciding factors in them signing for the club.

'Tactically, he wasn't one of those people who spend hours plotting their opponents' downfall; but he always knew the strengths and weaknesses of Newcastle's opponents in the Premier League. It was more often a case, though, of concentrating on his own team's strengths. He was always good at the backchat, the "We're better than they are!" He'd say things like, "Listen to what I'm saying to you in this dressing-room and imagine what their manager is saying to them in their dressing-room. They're frightened of us!"

'I'm sure he learned a lot from Shanks [Bill Shankly] and Bob Paisley. I think it's impossible not to learn from the people at Liverpool, because there's just so much common sense attached to what they've done. I think all the players that played there and have gone and had a dabble at management will always take with them a lot of what Liverpool do. It's inevitable.'

Whatever Keegan's strengths and weaknesses as a manager, there is no question that he will be remembered by all concerned with awe and affection for the dramatic changes he brought about at St James' Park. A blinkered obsession with attacking football, a suspect temperament and a failure to develop his playing staff outside the first-team squad pale into insignificance alongside the monumental achievement of transforming Newcastle United from Second Division relegation fodder into one of the leading, and most entertaining, clubs in the land inside five years.

'I think Kevin will always be remembered with huge affection and huge gratitude on Tyneside,' says John Gibson, 'because while Newcastle fans over the years have wanted to win things, they've always wanted to win them with style. Even if they didn't win things – and there were long periods when they didn't – they would say, "Ah, yes, but we've got Supermac [Malcolm Macdonald]!" They've always hung their hat on players with style – the Jimmy Smiths, the Macdonalds, the Tony Greens – and, all of a sudden, Keegan has brought a boat-load of them to the club. When his Newcastle were in form, when it worked, they were a joy to behold – something, in fact, I doubt we'll ever see again.

'Whatever Newcastle go on to do in terms of the championship, Keegan will never be forgotten because of the way he prevented the club from going into the Third Division and then took them to the top of the Premiership, smashing the transfer record time and time again to bring people like Ginola, Ferdinand and Shearer, at £15 million, to St James' Park.

'I think he was more charismatic than any other Newcastle United manager – he has played more adventurous football than any other Newcastle United manager – but he's also had more financial backing than any other Newcastle United manager. As you know, I've supported Newcastle since the fifties, and I don't think that, for sustained excitement, there's ever been anything to match Keegan's five years. I've never known anything like it. It was there when he was a player and it went to even greater heights when he was manager. Kevin was so different as a person to most people in football and was, therefore, so different as a manager.

'Yes, there was a tinge of bitterness that the man went out of the back door at the last minute without an explanation or a goodbye to the fans. I think that did sadden people enormously. He just went, and he's never come back; but that can't take away the overall picture of what the man achieved and the style of the man. There might only be a First Division championship standing to his name in the record books, but that doesn't begin to tell the story of what happened. It was the style and the pride that he gave Newcastle and their fans which will stand as his monument.'

Perhaps the final word on the subject should go to Sir John Hall. 'Kevin played the kind of football which was absolutely brilliant,' says the man whose money supplied the kind of players who made that style of play possible. 'The Keegan years, I think, will be remembered for that cavalier approach to football, a new approach to it. Just as we approached the challenge of reviving the club in a new business sense, he approached it with a new way of football. Maybe both of us were before our time in some ways. We didn't win anything, but we created something at the club. We created a club which everybody called "the entertainers" and everybody wanted to know. After Kevin said he was going, I said to him, "You know, I got hold of you to be one of the greatest managers in soccer!" And he said, "We'll never know, will we?"'

Or will we, given the developments at Craven Cottage, where Keegan has hitched his wagon to Mohammed Al Fayed, someone even richer than Sir John Hall, and started again to go through the gut-wrenching process of taking a club from the lower divisions up to the Premiership – albeit under the strange title of 'chief operations officer'.

12

THE GEORDIE NATION

Football is not a passion on Tyneside, it is a religion. Hardly an original way to put it, but there are not too many others to convey the overwhelming importance of Newcastle United in the life of the average Geordie. Almost certainly, the Newcastle fans would subscribe more readily than most to Bill Shankly's famous, over-the-top dictum that 'Football is not a matter of life and death, it's more important than that.' The supporters of other big clubs, like Manchester United and Liverpool, worship their heroes with real fervour; the supporters of Newcastle United do it with every fibre of their being. The results from St James' Park, dominating the sloping city from on high like some steel and concrete cathedral, do not make them merely happy or sad – they change their whole perspective on life.

The responses to a survey of Newcastle United fans conducted in 1995 reveal the extent to which the club dominates the lives of its adherents: 'I could not live without them; they are more important than life itself,' said an electrician in his twenties. Nor was that sense of hopeless addiction confined to blue-collar supporters. 'I spend more time talking, thinking, looking for news, anticipating, worrying, rejoicing, despairing and living Newcastle United than anything else in my life,' admitted an independent financial advisor in his thirties. 'My priorities in life are as follows: my wife, my career and NUFC. Thankfully, to date no one has ever asked me to put them in any particular order,' confessed a sales and marketing director in his thirties.

So, the magnetic, hypnotic pull of the club on the people of Tyneside is clearly classless. It appears to know no barriers of intellect or gender, either. 'Supporting Newcastle United is an essential part of my life,' declared a female student in that 1995 survey. 'It keeps me sane and is very enjoyable. Long may it last.' In many ways, the devotion the club receives from its flock is more Latin than English. When you search for a parallel you think first of places like Naples, where there is only one football club in a city which has experienced serious economic decline and deprivation. Thus, the club not only offers relief from the hardships of life, but also provides a focal point for the identity and aspirations of a region whose geographical remoteness from the rest of England gives it an almost insular mentality.

That is what Kevin Keegan knew instinctively and what he tapped into as both player and manager at Newcastle United. The 'Geordie nation' is how Sir John Hall has described the club's constituency and the separateness implicit in that title helps to explain why Newcastle United is such a unique corner of English football. When Keegan took over as manager in 1992, he knew the size of the job was magnified several thousand times by the yearning of the long-suffering fans for a team that not only played good football, but could also put the club back on the top shelf of English football.

He did all of that without actually winning anything, the First Division title excepted. So the leading question has to be, 'Were the Newcastle fans really satisfied with a team that promised so much and delivered so little? Is it true they wanted him to play attacking football as though there was no tomorrow?' It seems they were and it was. 'You can't argue with what Kevin did on the field,' says Steve Wraith. 'Basically, the fans had had nothing but doom and gloom for so long. I mean, it's well documented that they haven't won a major trophy for nearly forty years now.

'Those two years Kevin spent at Newcastle as a player were like a dream. Then we went through a period of decline. We knew we had a board of directors that we had to get rid of some way or another. Eventually we did that, but although we got rid of the directors, the players we had at the club still weren't good enough to do anything in that League. Kevin Keegan was probably the only man who, although he had no experience of that job at all, could come back as manager and inspire average players to play the way he used to.

'He made a start with attacking football and I don't think he could go back on that. Newcastle United made their mark as an attacking football team when they got promotion from the old Second Division; and when they got into the Premiership that first year, I think even Kevin got carried away with the "entertainers" tag Sky Sports gave them. Things started escalating from there. Kevin really did start to believe you could win things playing attacking football.

'His philosophy, he said, was to play the old Liverpool way – but you never saw Liverpool teams play the way Newcastle did under Keegan. Liverpool always passed from the back, and when things were going wrong they would take it back and start again. Kevin's team were going up the other end and scoring one or two, then conceding a couple before scoring a winner with a minute to go, which was fantastic entertainment. Even so, I think people reflect on Keegan's years as a dream world. At the end of the day, I think Kevin was living in a dream world because he didn't win anything, apart from promotion, with that kind of football.

'Attacking football is all very well, but I think it's finally been proved after five years that it doesn't win anything in the very top league, the Premiership. But they did their best. We had five glorious years under Kevin, and although there's a bitter taste in the mouth about the way he left, you could never take away from him the fact that he awoke the sleeping giant and put Newcastle United back on the map.'

Chris McMenemy, a Geordie himself, is acutely conscious of having been part of something special in the history of Newcastle United. 'You could see at first hand what it meant to the people in this area,' he says. 'It wasn't just a football match they were attending, it was a way of life. It is a big city and it didn't polarize people, it brought everybody together in a common aim. All of a sudden they had something to really believe in and it was something on their own doorsteps. It wasn't just that we were competing successfully with the big clubs, it was also the way that we did it. Newcastle had a history way back of having flamboyant players and Kevin had brought that back to them. He'd also given them a good chance of doing something over a longer period.'

It was the away games that really brought home to McMenemy the impact developments at St James' Park were having on the rest of the country and even further afield. 'We would take thousands of people abroad for our matches in Europe,' he marvels, 'and every club we played at in the Premier League had their biggest home gates. They loved having Newcastle in their town. The supporters had character and they had colour and they knew they were pleased to be there. We were everybody's second-favourite team. Everywhere you went – even abroad – there were black and white shirts.'

There was no more visible sign of the new self-belief engendered among the Geordies by Keegan's Newcastle than the proliferation of replica shirts throughout the city. 'I've never experienced a place that is so football-orientated,' said Mark Lawrenson after arriving there towards the end of 1996. 'I've never seen so many men in their thirties, forties and fifties walking round any town at any time of the day in the shirts of the local club. It's phenomenal, it really is. Football completely takes over.'

It wasn't always like that in the recent past, though. 'At one time,' says Steve Wraith, 'you wouldn't see a Newcastle United shirt in the city centre.' In fact, Wraith accuses his fellow-supporters of being fickle. 'Newcastle fans can't claim to be particularly loyal,' he argues. 'I remember a game against Oxford – I think it was in the Milk Cup, as the League Cup was called in the early eighties – that was abandoned at half-time because of fog, but we only had a crowd of 12,000, that was all. I felt embarrassed to be there. It was like, "Where's everybody else?" Another one that sticks in my mind is a friendly against Brondby. There was about 2500 there, pre-season.

'I remember that game in particular because I was actually standing in the Gallowgate corner at the time, me and my mates, when Liam O'Brien got the equalizer in a 2–2 draw. It was a comical goal – he chipped it over the goalkeeper, then got behind him and knocked it in with his knee. I remember we ran up and down trying to make it look as though there was a crowd there when it got covered on the local TV news. It was embarrassing in those days.'

The trouble with being a Newcastle fan is that there is no one else in the one-club city to have a go at. So the supporters direct their spleen at the next nearest clubs, Sunderland and Middlesbrough, and the club everyone loves to hate, Manchester United. That, in essence, was Wraith's answer when I asked him how he managed to make a success of his fanzine – by definition a critical publication – when Newcastle had been so successful over the past five years.

'Because Sunderland and Middlesbrough were so bad at the time and Manchester United were doing so well,' he said, 'we came up with a few gimmicks, like free gifts. They included Alex Ferguson toilet seat covers, so when the bonny lads came home on a Friday night after their lager and curry they could spew up all over Alex Ferguson's face; or there was the Peter Reid dartboard, where you could attach his picture over your existing board and get a double-top off Reid's forehead. That kind of thing – something you could have a laugh at, you know.'

While the *No. 9*'s sense of humour may be questionable, there is no doubting its commitment and sense of responsibility. 'We did criticize the club in our early days,' insists Wraith. 'I would say we are one of the four fanzines in the entire country who do criticize what the club does. For instance, the rise in season ticket prices is going to be at the forefront of the first issue this season [1997–98] because we are not happy about that. We were also part of the campaign against the banning of away fans from Newcastle–Sunderland derbies.

THE MAGNIFICENT OBSESSION

'Our feeling is that a lot of Newcastle fans are bandwagon jumpers. They just come along for the ride. Fair enough, they liked to support the club when Keegan was there. Before that, when they thought the club had no ambition, they walked away and came back when Keegan came back. These are the supporters we don't want at grounds.

'We get accused by some fans of being down on the club when it's successful, but if we don't have a go no one's going to do it and the club are going to get away with murder. They'll get away with murder anyway because the club has become a monster. They can steamroller everybody now; they've got no feelings for the supporters. They never did have, but they've got even less now. But there's nothing you can do about it.'

The question is, though, whether the Newcastle fans got the team they deserved. There is a school of thought that suggests they long only for the drama and excitement of cup football, as exemplified by the club's three FA Cup wins in the 1950s, and do not have the mental and emotional stamina for a title challenge over nine months. 'I remember sitting down with Arthur Cox one day,' recalls Mark Lawrenson, 'and he said, "It's funny you know, but Newcastle people, *en masse*, would rather Newcastle United win the FA Cup than the League because it's excitement, it's entertainment."'

Almost certainly, that predilection helped Kevin Keegan believe he was on the right lines when his team attacked everybody in sight. He gave the fans the excitement they craved, not with cup football but with the mundane, day-to-day fixtures of the Premier League. 'I'm sure that was all part of Kevin's ethos when he took over,' says Lawrenson. 'The players he bought meant that, whatever happened, they were going to have fun along the way and they were going to provide some entertainment.'

There was also the wider question of whether Newcastle United, under Keegan and Hall, provided a focal point for the economic and social regeneration of the area following the closure, mostly in the Thatcherite 1980s, of the pits and the shipyards which, traditionally, had supplied the people of the area with work and their predominantly masculine identity. Sir John, who describes himself as a 'capitalist with a social conscience', has never been in any doubt about it. 'When an area is fighting its way out of recession, as the North East was,' he says, 'you've got to break the cycle of decline, and I reckon Newcastle United did that.

'The club's success gave a kind of inspirational push to the region, and success breeds success. People need to have the confidence to believe in themselves. If you can get people to believe in themselves, you can do anything. I think we released that potential, which has always been here in the North East. When you get knocks from pit closures and the rest of it, you lose your confidence. You have got to get it back and I think the football club had a part in doing that and healing those wounds.

'Football is a global business and the publicity that soccer brings to a region, this region couldn't pay for; this free publicity is beyond the resources of the region – it brings more than economic benefits, gives people a quiet confidence again. When people come up to you and say, "Eh, marvellous. Tremendous what you do," that is the pride in the area coming out, and you cannot put a price on it.'

Many of the fans would agree. In the aforementioned 1995 survey, they voiced their views in a very positive manner. 'I think NUFC has become the focal point of the regeneration of the North East. It has given pride back and must be treated with care and sensitivity,' said a deputy headmaster in his fifties. 'From a business point of view,' added the managing director of one company, 'NUFC being in Europe this season helped put Newcastle on the map so far as our European customers were concerned.' But perhaps the most ringing endorsement came from a fire-fighter in his thirties. 'NUFC,' he said, 'is vitally important locally. It promotes our city elsewhere, improves our image (abroad for example) and also raises morale and puts a smile on faces. You only have to be out or at work after a good performance to notice this, as compared with a poor one.' A civil servant concluded, 'Given the loss of the area's traditional industries, the city and region need a focal point. NUFC provides this and also generates an image beyond the region.'

Sir John Hall's own feeling is that the area has to rid itself of its inferiority complex. 'The people of the North East have always been very introverted,' he asserts. 'They have wondered who was going to help them. We've got to get over that and learn sense. For too long we dwelt in the past. If you live in the past, you die in the past. We don't do that any more – we are a successful region. We fought our battles and that needs to be recognized. I look forward to the day when we have some form of regionalism, but I don't want to see another elected assembly, which would be just another extension of the Labour government.

'There is tremendous success which has been built upon the partnership between the private sector, the trade unions and the public sector, and we all have something to offer. But if the politicians get in they will just pick away at the private sector and I think we would end up as we were. So if we can keep the partnership in some form, that will be good for the region.'

Hall says helping to regenerate the region was one of the reasons he branched out into other sports. His first step was to buy the Durham Wasps ice hockey team in 1995. Then, later the same year, he snapped up the major local rugby union club, Newcastle Gosforth, renamed them the Newcastle Falcons and brought in former England fly half Rob Andrew as managing director on a five-year contract worth £750,000. Typically, where the innovative Sir John is concerned, they were Britain's first full-time professional rugby union club and he was in on the ground floor as this most amateur of sports awkwardly embraced professionalism.

Subsequently, a basketball team, the Newcastle Eagles, and a motor racing team, Lister Storm, were added to the stable. Although the motor racing team, based in Surrey, does not have

'Newcastle' in its title, the cars carry those distinctive black and white stripes and the club crest when they race at Daytona and Le Mans. As for the Eagles, they play at the new, multi-purpose Newcastle Arena on the banks of the Tyne, as do the ice hockey team, now known as the Cobras.

Explaining the purpose behind this sporting empire, Sir John says, 'As I travelled round Europe on a fact-finding trip, I was influenced in Spain and Portugal by the sporting clubs. They were the idea of the old Fascist governments in the 1930s and were intended, in my view, to take the people's minds off revolution. The governments built the stadiums and handed them over to the municipalities. The clubs that used them were like the old rugby clubs, where the members paid so much a year to belong. You then gained subsidies from the local authorities, and that's how the whole thing was put together. That's how most of them still are on the Continent and I like the idea of being able to go down and play basketball, ice hockey, tennis or football when you are members and it's a family atmosphere.'

Hall admits to having been particularly impressed by the wide range of sporting facilities available to the 105,000 members of Barcelona football club. 'They carry that badge – the Barcelona badge – with pride,' he says of the membership, 'and I thought to myself, "We have got that at Newcastle. We have got a tremendous monopoly, a tremendous tradition of sport. If I put it together and get at the sports, I've got the software for future television coverage of sport. That's the business side of it. Everybody's doing it now, but I saw this years ago – this is the way forward. But I also wanted to capitalize on the North East's tradition of sport and have the sporting club, because if you can create champions, success breeds success.'

There is another, hard-headed reason for the expansion of the sporting empire. Since the population of Newcastle is only 250,000, the Halls are keen to increase the catchment area around the city and appeal to a much wider audience in the North East. 'Certain people will not invest in Newcastle United because of regional competition from Sunderland and

Middlesbrough [football clubs], but they might invest in ice hockey or basketball,' Douglas Hall was quoted as saying in 1996. 'Our initial catchment area is the North East, about 1.5 million people,' said his father a year later, 'and then we've got to spread the net further, worldwide, and that's our next plan.'

Whether there is any direct correlation between sporting success and the undeniable economic revival in the North East is difficult to assess. Needless to say, the city's plentiful pubs and clubs do even more of a roaring trade than usual when United win, while the wide choice of shopping centres and restaurants benefits from the large numbers of visiting fans drawn to Newcastle by the football. Every year, for instance, Scandinavians come over in their hundreds of thousands on cheap weekend package trips combining shopping and football. The only threat to that lucrative trade is the scarcity of tickets for St James' Park, so they might have to settle for Sunderland or Middlesbrough instead.

The only truly tangible evidence of football bringing jobs to the area was the decision by Samsung, the South Korean electronics giant, to build a new factory on land within Sir John's capacious Wynyard Hall Estate. Seemingly, what persuaded Samsung to ignore attractive offers to site the factory in other parts of the country was the promise of an executive box at St James' Park when Kevin Keegan's team were in full, majestic flow. 'Everything else had to be right for Samsung – the site, the workforce, the communications,' said Michael Mitchell, of the North East Chamber of Commerce, 'but United was the icing on the cake; and if that swung it, why not?'

Trading links with northern Spain, too, were established through the football club. When Newcastle played the second, away leg of their otherwise disastrous UEFA Cup tie against Athletic Bilbao in 1994, Sir John arranged for a delegation of local businessmen to accompany the team on their charter flight. It is also true that Newcastle United were included as a senior partner when the city council were working on an economic regeneration strategy that same year. 'The club is a symbol of excellence for this town, no question,' Tony Flynn, leader of the council, was quoted as saying in 1996, 'but you have to build on it. I don't want to make too strong a comparison with Liverpool, but a successful football team doesn't necessarily mean you'll automatically get a successful town.' Michael Mitchell agreed. 'You have to work at it,' he said. 'Anything that raises the profile of the city we will exploit.'

Not a trick was missed off the field, certainly, when Barcelona came to town for Newcastle's first match in the Champions League in September 1997. Before visiting journalists went out to report what proved to be a thrilling game and a stunning 3–2 victory for Newcastle, they were handed a publicity pack extolling the virtues and attractions of the city. In an introductory letter Tony Flynn said, 'On behalf of the people of Newcastle, the City Council would like to extend a warm welcome to all journalists, photographers and camera crews covering United's Champions League match with Barcelona. As well as its passion for football, Newcastle is famed for its architecture, nightlife and the friendliness of its citizens. I hope you will have a chance to experience all this during your stay, but if not I would love to see you visit us again in the not too distant future.'

The message itself may have been unremarkable, but what made the pack unusual was its very existence. Speaking as a football writer who has travelled extensively during the past thirty years, I have often experienced something similar at big games or tournaments abroad; but it's an uncommon experience to come across it in England. The pack even contained a scaled-down version of one of a series of posters sponsored by Newcastle Brown Ale for the Year of Visual Arts in the north of England 1996 'In celebration of Newcastle United supporters who have carried their team forward in the race to the top of the Premier League'. It shows a crowd of Newcastle fans in a pub either rueing a miss or suffering a goal against, as they often did towards the end of that galling 1996–97 season. And just guess what legend is written around the edge of the picture? Yes, 'Football isn't a matter of life and death . . .'

THE MAGNIFICENT OBSESSION

There is no doubt whatsoever that Keegan and Hall put Newcastle back on the map, made the city's name known around the world; and that cannot have done any harm in commercial terms. Terry Cooney, the Labour councillor and Newcastle fan, remembers being reminded of the fact in unexpected circumstances. 'It was last year [1996],' he says, 'and I was over in Amsterdam at a worldwide conference as chairman of the emergency planning committee of the Tyne and Wear Fire Authority. I was having a meal and it turned out that the fellow sitting next to me was from Peru. He knew I was from England – though not from which part – and while we are chatting away, he says, "Oh, yes, I watch the English football, you know, on Sky. I must admit the football I do enjoy most is the Premier League and the club that I really enjoy watching is Keegan's Newcastle United." Now that was a comment by someone from South America, where they have seen the likes of Pele so they know the football world. As I've said before many times, Newcastle United are great ambassadors for the city. Keegan has done all that, and you cannot take it away from him.'

Not *everyone* on Tyneside is infatuated with Newcastle United and Sir John Hall, however. Their plans to build first a £15 million ice rink and arena and then a £65 million, 55,000-seater football stadium in Leazes Park, right next to St James' Park, have stirred up what the *Guardian* called 'an alliance of pinkish middle classes, conservation groups and disaffected Labour councillors in a Labour city'. An unexpectedly powerful alliance it turned out to be, too. To the embarrassment of the leaders of the council, who had backed the idea, the planning committee vetoed the ice rink/arena by ten votes to six.

Emboldened by that success, the protesters put up a really fierce fight against the proposed new football stadium. At the start of 1997 they had collected nearly 22,000 signatures on a petition (more than ten times the number they got when opposing the ice rink/arena) and they were parading every day in Northumberland Street, Newcastle's main thoroughfare, waving placards that proclaimed that the football club was becoming too self-important.

That feeling of resentment – jealousy even – looks to be an important element in the barricade of opposition to Newcastle United's plans for expansion. Sir John and his cohorts have been successful on such a grand scale that there is obviously a worry in some quarters it may not be long before they take over the city completely. While the protesters argue legitimately that Leazes Park is a conservation area entrusted to the council by the old freemen of the city and protected by ancient statute, you cannot help but suspect some of them just want to see Hall and United cut down to size.

As Dolly Potter, the retired inspector of historical buildings who chaired the Friends of Leazes Park Committee, said after the ice rink/arena plan had been torpedoed, 'Lots of people have offered me congratulations. They said he [Sir John Hall] got a slap in the face, that he was getting too big for his boots, but I don't want to be seen to be anti-Newcastle United.'

Another revealing quote came from Dave Clelland, the MP for Tyne Bridge, in 1996 when he was discussing the heavy involvement of Cameron Hall Developments and Shepherd Offshore in Tyne Port 2000, a private consortium bidding for the profitable Port of Tyne Authority. Clelland, a former leader of Gateshead Council, which gave Sir John approval for his Metro Centre, said, 'No question about the success of the football club and hats off to everyone, particularly Kevin Keegan. But I do have concerns about the continued expansion of the empire. There's a limit to what people in this region think wise about the power wielded by one person, or a number of people – I don't think it's healthy for a small group of people to expand to the extent that they're in control of a large sector of services.'

There was no disguising the disappointment and frustration felt by Hall at running into such obdurate opposition over the proposed new stadium. It was even more irritating for him that his alternative plan of a move to Gateshead had been scuppered by Newcastle's own fans. 'There's a lot of flak about this,' he said, 'but we have it down on record that I would have gone to Gateshead. Gateshead Council has tremendous enthusiasm for sport, and I wanted to go there. The site was there – a difficult site, admittedly – and I just felt that people would have supported a winning Newcastle United wherever the new stadium was built.

'But Newcastle City Council said we had to stay in the city, and so did the fans. So we looked at sites in Newcastle – the city council had fourteen of them – and it seemed that the one in Leazes Park was probably the one that would satisfy the councillors most. The new stadium is not going to be on the park; it's on wasteland [a claim challenged strongly by the conservationists] and we put together a scheme which I believe was a good one. But there is a lot of opposition from people, although I don't know who they are – people of the city or people from outside.

'There is a lot of unfair criticism, but it is a democratic process, as I have told them. We have the right, democratically, to make a planning application and we have the right democratically to object. The council have got to decide, although it will most probably go to a public inquiry and, at the end of the day, they will say yes or no. I have decided that I will have to accept the democratic decision of the Minister, but it doesn't alter the fact that we need another stadium, a bigger stadium, to compete with the likes of Manchester United. If we have crowds of 36,000 every week for Premiership football, we'll need 50–60,000 for European football. The kids shouldn't have to go to cinemas [to watch live, closed-circuit TV transmissions of Newcastle United matches] but there just aren't the seats to accommodate everybody.

'Kids come here and say, "We canna get tickets, can you help us?" He's standing there, a fanatical young kid, and he hasn't seen a live match. That's awful. We can't afford to lose them and we've got pressure from the press asking what we are going to do about the kids. So when we look to see what we can do, we get criticized for wanting to build a new stadium. We've got huge waiting lists, and unless we build a new stadium we are going to kill off the next generation of fans.'

Given all the controversy the proposed new stadium has caused, Hall bitterly regrets not having persuaded the old board to build one at Gateshead back in the 1980s. 'One of the things I said years ago,' he recalls, 'was that we should have built a new stadium at the Metro Centre, on the land that was available there. But I got criticized for trying to move the situation. The Metro Centre was in an enterprise zone, though, and the club could have got cheap money and tax benefits because of it. It was before I got on the board, and I was attacked by Stan Seymour [a former chairman]. He, the press and the fans asked what on earth I was trying to do. They didn't understand what I was talking about. They didn't understand you've got to build new stadiums.

'What I feel I'm good at is looking ahead and trying to guide, but the difficult part is getting people to follow you, and in football, you haven't got the time to hang around. We at Newcastle have still got a long way to make up, but we're getting there. We're a very, very ambitious club, and that ambition hasn't gone.'

13

THE FUTURE

Only a gifted psychic could have predicted at the very start of 1997 that Newcastle United would have to face the future a year later without both Kevin Keegan and Sir John Hall, the partnership that had led them out of the wilderness and into the promised land. While not entirely unexpected on Tyneside, Keegan's resignation on 8 January came as a major shock to the rest of the country. Similarly, those unaware of Sir John's growing disenchantment with the burdens of office were taken aback by the announcement, on 15 September, that he was to retire as chairman of the club at the end of the year.

So where do Newcastle United go from here without the two men who have made them what they are? On the field, it looks as though it could be on to greater glory. As expected, Kenny Dalglish has made Newcastle harder to beat; without robbing them of that attacking brio which distinguished their football under Keegan. At the time of writing, they had made a steady start to the Premiership season and their astounding victory over Barcelona in the Champions League had suggested that Dalglish had more than come to terms with the complexities of European football.

It was an achievement made all the more remarkable by the loss of Alan Shearer shortly before the start of the 1997-98 season due to a serious ankle injury. The irony was that Dalglish, supposedly a Cromwellian leader, replaced Shearer very effectively with Faustino Asprilla, the Colombian cavalier who had been looked upon as one of the luxury items in Keegan's outlay of £60 million on new players. Never mind all the goals

Asprilla scored as a lone striker, including a hat-trick against Barcelona that will stay in the memory for ever – the work-rate and dedication Dalglish got out of him were a tribute to both player and manager.

In playing terms, therefore, Newcastle looked none the worse for Keegan's departure. In point of fact, it seemed as though their chances of winning something at long last might have been improved by Dalglish's unwillingness to follow Keegan's example of gambling everything on attack. 'Kenny's just making sure they are difficult to beat,' observed Mark Lawrenson. 'He knows what they can do going forward and he knows it's a case of getting the balance right. He just goes about his way. That's the way he is.'

Derek Fazackerley was more reluctant to comment, but there was no denying the accuracy of his predictions. Speaking before Dalglish started wielding the axe, Keegan's former chief coach said, 'It's not for me to say how Kenny has changed things tactically, but Peter Beardsley probably won't see the season out, nor David Ginola. So, straight away, they've gone through the flair players, if you like, and put the more reliable type of player in. They are probably a little bit stronger, and more efficient at scratching results when they are not playing well.'

Even so, without Keegan, some vital spark was missing from the equation. It was as if a torrid love affair between fans and manager had been replaced by a marriage of convenience. Steve Wraith, who had reported signs of a warming towards Dalglish at the end of the 1996–97 season, was less hopeful about the relationship four months later. 'With Dalglish,' he said, 'we still find it hard to accept the fact that Keegan's gone. A lot of the songs at the ground were based around Kevin Keegan's black and white army and the chant of "Kee-gan" used to resound round the ground. Dalglish's name still doesn't echo round St James' Park or round the fans at away games like that yet. I think people are still trying to come to terms with Kevin's departure. So maybe his going to Fulham will bring the Geordies into reality and make them realize he has actually gone.'

THE FUTURE

However, Derek Fazackerley doubts whether anyone will ever be able to establish the same kind of close relationship with the Newcastle supporters. 'Kevin and Kenny are totally different personalities,' he says. 'Kenny's rapport with the fans will be built up purely on the success of the football team, whereas I don't think Kevin necessarily had to win anything to have the same rapport. They adored him as a person: he was a very open person and they felt he was one of them. I don't think they'll ever get that close to Kenny – he's a more private person.

'He wants to be a winner, like Kevin, but he goes about it in a different way. When I was there, we'd get 2–3000 people watching the training sessions. Kevin used to love that, but it's not something Kenny would encourage. So, straight away, there's that distance between Kenny and the public. They'll give him a fair chance to give them a successful football team, but the relationship, the bond, will never, ever be the same as it was with Kevin – even if Kenny wins something. Except that he'll have done it his way and they'll be pleased about that.'

Not surprisingly, then, one thing Wraith was able to knock firmly on the head was any suggestion that Keegan's surprising decision to return to football with Fulham had triggered a sense of outrage and betrayal among the Newcastle supporters. 'The relationship between Kevin and the fans remains as strong as ever,' he insisted. 'A lot's been made of the fact that he never intended to come back into football in the first place and people have been bringing up the old quote about him saying Newcastle was the only job he would have come back for. But Newcastle fans aren't that naive. They realized that Kevin Keegan would come back into it again. He just needed a rest.

'A lot of the tabloids have tried to get people to speak out and the TV programmes up here have been full of it – vox pops, people going on to the streets and asking them if they feel betrayed by Kevin. One or two have said, "Yes, it's ridiculous", but others have said, "Yes, he deserves to have had a rest, and if he wants to go back into the game, then let him get on with it." There's no degree of hatred, no sense of betrayal up here or anything. If Kevin comes back to St James' Park at any time, he'll get a fantastic reception. Kevin, out of all the Newcastle United legends who are still alive, has taken over the old mantle of Stan Seymour – he is Mr Newcastle now.'

An intelligent and articulate young man, Wraith has a couple of interesting theories of his own about Keegan. One concerns his past, the other his future. 'Personally speaking, I'm not surprised Kevin has taken the Fulham job,' said Wraith. 'He's one of the few, like Brian Clough, you would expect to be involved in the game until they couldn't go on any longer. I'm just tinged with disappointment in that I wish he'd gone to Fulham, or somewhere like it, before he came to Newcastle. Maybe he could have learned the pressures of football management, gained that little bit of experience and then come to Newcastle and probably been able to win some honours for the fans.

'The game will be a lot better for him coming back into it, and I do feel he will eventually end up managing at international level. If Glenn Hoddle fails to get England to the World Cup finals, or decides to call it a day for some reason, I'm sure somewhere along the line Kevin and the likes of Ray Wilkins will be involved. After all, both have already had a taste of it with the Under-21s. I think Kevin realizes that the only way he will actually gain any recognition with the FA and any chance of getting to the top level is by going back into the game. I think he's realized he has to learn a lot at the lower levels as well as at the higher levels.'

One thing the departures of Keegan and Hall will definitely leave Newcastle without is a natural spokesman. Although towards the end of his chairmanship Sir John came to resent the insatiable demands of the media for information and comment, there was nothing he relished more than speaking up for his club and the 'Geordie nation' when confronted by tape recorders, microphones and cameras. Similarly, Keegan may have gone into his shell after blowing that twelve-point lead in the Premiership, but he remains one of the most fluent and charismatic communicators football has ever seen.

THE FUTURE

In terms of public relations alone Newcastle United were extremely fortunate to have had both of them on board at the same time. Their willingness to go out and meet the fans face-to-face, or to give the local and national press a good headline, was almost as important to the revival of Newcastle United as anything achieved on the field of play. So it will be extremely difficult to compensate for the loss of them both inside a year, especially as there would appear to be no natural successors among the remaining administrative and managerial cast at St James' Park.

Since Kenny Dalglish joined Newcastle, he has been noticeably less prickly, laconic and evasive than he used to be in his public pronouncements. Despite this welcome improvement in his communication skills, however, that sometimes impenetrable Glaswegian accent of his would not appeal to many if they had to choose a spokesman. Nor has Douglas Hall inherited his father's liking for the spotlight. Both Hall Jnr, who is to become vice-chairman, and the new chairman-elect, Freddie Shepherd, prefer to stay in the background. So it looks as though the burden of representing the club in public will fall mainly on the talkative and knowledgeable chief executive, Freddie Fletcher.

He could have quite a lot of talking to do, given the controversy raging over the new stadium and the long delay there has been in getting started on the £15 million, state-of-the-art training complex and youth academy Newcastle plan to build near Newcastle Airport, in the north-western outskirts of the city. Sir John, whose pride and joy the project is, seems to have been enthusing about it ever since he became chairman – yet not one sod has so far been turned on the 315-acre site. 'We've got planning permission,' he explained, 'but the detail on it is very complicated. The airport needs some land because they are extending, so we are having to work that out with them. But we need training facilities of our own, we need an academy and we're determined.'

If and when it is built, the complex will comprise a training ground for the senior players, a 'centre of excellence' for young

181

footballers, a department specializing in sports medicine and a golf course. Sir John believes it will not only enable Newcastle to harvest the rich crop of gifted young players the North East traditionally produces – rather than letting them slip away elsewhere, as has too often been the case in the past – but also give the first team an advantage over their rivals in the annual battle for the game's highest honours.

'There's very little difference between the top six clubs in our football,' Sir John said, 'and I think you'll find in a number of years that you need to get an edge. That edge, I reckon, will come from sports medicine and science and training and fitness. So we've got to build up much more than we've ever done, and football's got to recognize that it doesn't know all about fitness. It's advancing to a level now which they've got to recognize. I see in the future big departments of sports medicine and science at clubs, with experts coming in, looking at the players and getting them fit through pre-season training, daily training, injury care, diets and psychology.

'We've done it by the seat of our pants for years, but it has become more refined and knowledgeable than it's ever been and we've got to tap into it. It means big departments, so you are looking at big investments. But that's what any business has to do – it has to invest in research and development. If it doesn't, it will die, and we're no different. I don't think enough people have sat down and thought it through about the way soccer's going to develop in the future. Getting the intellectual argument over about the game's future development is very difficult and very frustrating, I find.'

Now that Newcastle United are a public limited company, all this talk of big investments clearly perplexed the money men in the City of London. They looked at the pre-tax loss of £23.6 million that Newcastle's last available accounts showed for the 1995–96 season and wondered how on earth they were going to be able to fund a new £65 million stadium and a £15 million training complex. However, that loss is accounted for

THE FUTURE

by expenditure of £27.6 million on transfer fees, which included the then world record sum of £15 million they paid Blackburn for Alan Shearer. Not only have Newcastle stopped buying on such a grand scale, knowing the first two stages of their regeneration plan are over, but Dalglish's wheeling and dealing has actually brought millions back into the club and cut the annual wage bill which, at more than £19 million, was the biggest in English football.

Newcastle United's earning potential is also enormous. Already, after only five years of reconstruction, their annual turnover is nearly £29 million a year, which puts them second only to Manchester United – who have had a lot longer to build up to £50 million-plus – among the Premier League clubs. The commercial side of the business is certainly booming. They have sold something like two and a half million replica shirts around the world in the past five years. When a new shirt came out at the start of the 1997–98 season, they shifted more than £1.7 million's worth in the first three months. This is a staggering amount of money.

As Chris McMenemy observed, 'I don't think there's many other clubs in the country who could possibly have the basis to try and catch Manchester United, with their ten-year start in terms of planning and structure. The fan base is there, the finances now look to be in place and the stadium will be even bigger; so they'll probably have the chance to go and do that. This club could get so big. You hope it would never go the other way, the way it used to be under the old board, but I don't think it will.'

The runners-up spot in the Premiership that Newcastle pinched from under the noses of Arsenal and Liverpool in 1996–97 also helped to establish the Tyneside club as the second biggest in England. Their immediate financial reward for qualifying for the revamped Champions League was a minimum of £7 million that should help to allay the fears of the City about Newcastle's ability to pay their way. It is a measure of the enormous strides the club has made under Sir John Hall, Kevin

THE MAGNIFICENT OBSESSION

Keegan and Kenny Dalglish that that was about the size of Newcastle's debt in 1992, when the great adventure began. So there is no reason for the future to be faced with anything but confidence.